NEW BATS
IN
OLD BELFRIES

'*Sumer is icumen in*', *Uffington 1935*, by Osbert Lancaster; the performers of the round are (*left to right*) Lord Berners (*piano*), Maurice Bowra, Adrian Bishop (*behind Bowra*), Karen Lancaster, John Betjeman, Osbert Lancaster (*flute*), Penelope Betjeman (*guitar*)

NEW BATS IN OLD BELFRIES

or

SOME LOOSE TILES

Maurice Bowra

Edited by Henry Hardy and Jennifer Holmes

With an introduction by Julian Mitchell

RD

ROBERT DUGDALE

in association with Wadham College

OXFORD

2005

Robert Dugdale, 26 Norham Road, OXFORD, OX2 6SF

ISBN-13: 978-0-946976-11-9
ISBN-10: 0-946976-11-2

Design by Bob Elliott
Proof-reading by Myra Jones
Production control by Adrian Bullock
Typeset in Minion by Deltatype Ltd, Birkenhead, Merseyside
Printed and bound in Great Britain by
Biddles Ltd, King's Lynn, Norfolk

To the memory of Eroica Rawbum

ne diu taceat procax
Fescennina iocatio . . .[1]

[1] 'Let not the saucy Fescennine jesting be long silent.' Catullus
61. 119–20. The Latin original was written by John Sparrow (with
'nec' for 'ne') on the front free endpaper of the first volume of the
manuscript of the poems. 'Fescennine' means scurrilous and
obscene.

Contents

¹ This and the next poem but one have been omitted for reasons explained in the preface (see p. xiii below).

Editorial preface

HENRY HARDY

MAURICE BOWRA's often extremely bawdy poems have long been
famous in certain circles, partly for being unpublished.[1] As John
Sparrow, one of Bowra's most intimate friends (and his literary
executor), used to say, it was a pity that Maurice had cut himself
off from posterity: 'his prose was unreadable and his verse was
unprintable'.[2]

The poems first came to my attention through Isaiah Berlin,
another of their author's (and Sparrow's) close friends, whose
writings I have been editing on and off for the last thirty years.
Berlin and Sparrow had started making notes on them, identifying
various people referred to, sometimes obliquely, by Bowra; they
had it in mind to annotate the text sufficiently to make the poems
comprehensible to readers not already able to understand the many
allusions they contain – allusions which are becoming increasingly
obscure as time goes by. Unfortunately, though, both Berlin and
Sparrow died before much progress had been made. It seemed to
me desirable to complete this work, not only because it was one of
Berlin's literary projects, but for its own sake. Publication was the
obvious next step, though it is unclear whether this was in the

---

[1] Some of them have in fact appeared in part, or in one case complete but
separately (a procedure reminiscent of the Oxford definition of a secret as 'Something
you tell only one person at a time'). Noel Annan, in 'A Man I Loved', in Hugh Lloyd-
Jones (ed.), *Maurice Bowra: A Celebration* [hereafter *Celebration*], 1974, 78–81, quotes
two stanzas of 'A Young Man and Old', part III; three stanzas of 'Old Mortality'
(repeated in his *The Dons: Mentors, Eccentrics and Geniuses*, 1999, 165); and most of the
first two parts of 'Old Croaker'. Six lines of the latter poem are also quoted by
Elizabeth Longford, *The Pebbled Shore: The Memoirs of Elizabeth Longford*, 1986, 73–4.
In *The Letters of Ann Fleming*, ed. Mark Amory, 1985, 231 note 3, the editor gives us the
first stanza of 'Prize Song'; Bevis Hillier follows suit in *John Betjeman: New Fame, New
Love*, 2002, 610, and also prints, as an appendix (612–15), the whole of 'Uffington
Downs', extracts from which had previously been included by Betjeman's daughter,
Candida Lycett Green, in her edition of her father's *Letters*, vol. 1, *1926 to 1951*, 1994,
137. A. L. Rowse includes two stanzas from 'Old Mortality' and two extracts from the
first part of 'Old Croaker', doubtless drawn from Annan's piece, in a chapter on Bowra
in his *Friends and Contemporaries*, 1989, 93–4.

[2] *Celebration*, 76.

minds of the original editors, who almost certainly felt more cautious, partly because more of the poems' subjects were alive when they were considering how to proceed.

Many of those who have read the poems (myself included) think them remarkable and *sui generis*. The best of them are surely masterpieces of their admittedly slight kind: impressively learned, full of literary echoes, sparklingly witty, as well as unashamedly lewd and scurrilous; and the versification is often exhilarating. It is important to add that they certainly weren't intended to be taken as true reports of what they sometimes 'allege'; nor do they read as if they were. Many of the poems could be described only loosely as being 'about' their subjects at all: rather they are highly inventive flights of fancy, fantastical elaborations constructed on slender, if any, veridical foundations, even if a small kernel of fact does sometimes give a special piquancy to the fictive superstructure. But this is not the place to enter into a critical assessment: for that, readers are referred to the illuminating introduction by Julian Mitchell, who is perhaps uniquely well equipped to provide the commentary the work requires.

The dedication

I owe the form of the dedication to Patrick Leigh Fermor, who wrote to me apropos Bowra's sensitivity to (implied) criticism: 'Playing paper-games one evening [in Greece], we tried making anagrams out of the names of friends, and ours. I came up with Eroica Rawbum for Maurice, and, when I read it out, there was a quick flicker of vexation followed by a cheery laugh: "Yerss, yerss, and very raw it is" – and a change of theme.'[1]

Excisions

The list of those accorded the Bowra treatment includes many of the best-known names of the twentieth century, including (for example) Isaiah Berlin, John Betjeman, Kenneth Clark, Rosamond Lehmann, Goronwy Rees, A. L. Rowse and Harold Macmillan. Many of Bowra's victims (Betjeman for one) were shown the poems, and some of them were delighted by what they read. But not all Bowra's subjects have felt flattered by their appearance in

---

[1] Letter of 29 November 2004.

his *galère*. For that reason I have consulted all living persons who are identifiably mentioned, lest some among them might not wish references to themselves to appear in the published text. I should like to thank those who agreed, sometimes with understandable reservations, to let 'their' poems stand. Two of those still living as I write this demurred, and the relevant poems have been omitted, or a name cut, accordingly. However, spaces of the right size have been left for the excised matter to be restored in future impressions if minds or circumstances change.

Editorial matters

I have silently corrected most of Bowra's surprisingly numerous spelling errors, and lightly modernised some of his punctuation, to avoid distracting readers with insubstantial eccentricity of this kind. Three poems found among Bowra's papers that seemed to belong with the ones Bowra himself included in the canon, and one poem of the same genre from Isaiah Berlin's papers, have been added as an appendix.

Where different texts of poems exist, an attempt has been made to identify Bowra's latest intentions, and to follow them. This question arises because Bowra's papers contain early drafts of some of the satires, and because he copied out some of them for his friends, either collectively in his own hand in a presentation volume, or on a typewriter one at a time, or in letters. Bowra evidently continued working on the poems as he copied them out, and the surviving texts differ here and there, usually but not always trivially. Almost always the principal manuscript – written in Bowra's hand in two bound volumes now held by the Codrington Library at All Souls College in Oxford, where they were placed by John Sparrow – appears to offer the latest and best text. But in the case of one poem, 'Lord Boothby Enters Heaven', we have followed another version, in which the differences struck us as improvements – perhaps Bowra typed out this text of the poem some time after it was written, polishing it further in the process. For this version we are indebted to Sylvester Gates's son Oliver Gates, who kindly made available to us both a volume[1] of selected poems

---

[1] This volume, which uses the subtitle of the Codrington manuscript (and of the present volume) as its main title, and vice versa, bears a dedication to Pauline and Sylvester Gates.

written up to 1941, copied out by Bowra in an order rather different from that in which they appear in the main manuscript, and a number of later poems typed out on separate sheets and sent to Sylvester Gates at various times.

The annotation requires a few words of explanation. In many cases the first note to a poem provides background information relevant to the poem as a whole, partly to avoid the need for multiple and repetitive notes on specific points; these opening notes, unnumbered to avoid defacing the titles of the poems with note cues, are preceded by the symbol § and followed by a small space so that they stand out more clearly from the remaining notes. There are also a few conventions that should be mentioned: all Oxford colleges except New College are referred to without the word 'College',[1] and University College is 'Univ.'; information in the form 'Balliol classics 1929–33' indicates that the person concerned was an undergraduate reading that subject at that Oxford college during that period; cross-references of the form '(56/6)' mean 'see page 56, note 6' (§ refers to an opening note of the kind described above); books are referred to on first mention by full title and date of first publication, subsequently just by (short) title, with a cross-reference to the note in which the full title appears (except in the case of the frequently cited *Celebration* and *Memories*, xi/1 and xviii/1); page references are given as numerals unprefixed by 'p.'.

Acknowledgements

I am most grateful to Wadham College, who own the copyright in the poems, for allowing me to publish them at last, forty years after the most recent one was written. All income from sales, after the deduction of publication expenditure, will go to the College for development purposes. I have had constant support, help and advice from Cliff Davies, Keeper of the Archives, and the benefit of the legal expertise of Jeffrey Hackney (Acting Warden at the time in question) in agreeing formal terms with the College.

I also thank Julian Mitchell for his truly excellent introduction, and for a great deal of knowledgeable help during the preparation of the edition. Leslie Mitchell, Bowra's official biographer, has

---

[1] Note that Christ Church is not properly known as Christ Church College.

generously shared his knowledge with me too; some of this derives from the work done towards such a biography by Michael Davie before ill-health led him to abandon the project.

Virtually all the research for and drafting of the footnotes was undertaken by my co-editor Jennifer Holmes, whose exceptional abilities and high standards are already known to me, to my good fortune, from her work on Isaiah Berlin's letters. In this case her main problem has been to track down private information, which has meant immersing herself in the biographies, autobiographies and collections of letters relating to Bowra's circle of friends, in order to identify the full cast of the poems, and the personal traits or sets of circumstances that sparked off Bowra's inventions. Despite our best efforts, some of Bowra's allusions remain obscure, and are therefore left unannotated here. If any reader can throw further light where it remains to be shed, we shall be grateful for the illumination, and readers of future impressions will benefit accordingly (please write to Henry Hardy at Wolfson College, OXFORD, OX2 6UD, *henry.hardy@wolfson.ox.ac.uk*). Help of this kind from Brigid Allen, Simon Bailey, Oliver Gates, Simon Green, Ian Harris, Bevis Hillier, Leofranc Holford-Strevens, James Morwood, John Penney, Jon Stallworthy and Mary Yoe, to whom we are duly grateful, has already been incorporated.

Jennifer and I have depended on the generous help given us by a number of archivists who have been able to supplement the resources of Wadham College: in Oxford Judith Curthoys (Christ Church), Robin Darwall-Smith (Magdalen), Clare Hopkins (Trinity), Alan Tadiello (Balliol) and Jennifer Thorp (New College); elsewhere Suzanne Foster (Winchester College), Christine Leighton (Cheltenham College) and Eddie Smith (Westminster School).

I am grateful to Professor Ian Maclean, Fellow Librarian at All Souls, for allowing me to consult the Codrington volumes, and to reproduce facsimiles therefrom in this one; the facsimiles were kindly made by the Librarian in Charge, Dr Norma Aubertin-Potter, on the Codrington's scanner. I have followed the order of the poems in this MS, which is not always strictly chronological, though it may be that Bowra arranged some or all of them in the order in which they were first drafted.

The two drawings by Osbert Lancaster are reproduced (one on the jacket, one as a frontispiece) by kind permission of Lady

Lancaster,[1] from scans helpfully provided by John R. Murray. I am grateful to Chris McDowell, Librarian of Newsquest (Oxfordshire) Ltd, for making it possible for me to use the photograph of Bowra at Wadham on the back of the jacket; this is a detail from a photograph published in the *Oxford Times* on 1 October 1953, to mark the opening of what is now called the Goddard Building, after its architect.

Two former colleagues from my distant-seeming Oxford University Press years (1977–90), Adrian Bullock and Bob Elliott, have stepped into the two main breaches in my publishing expertise – production and design respectively – to very satisfying effect. Douglas Matthews, who has compiled the majority of my Berlinian indexes, has kindly made this one too. What if anything it is that I have myself contributed to the project (apart from an obstinate determination to see it come to fruition) now escapes me; but I am delighted to witness its completion, and I hope that the final product will give many people much pleasure, and none pain.

HENRY HARDY

Wolfson College, Oxford
May 2005

---

[1] The drawing on the jacket appears in her late husband's book *With an Eye to the Future*, 1967, 71; the frontispiece has been published in Bevis Hillier, *John Betjeman: A Life in Pictures*, 1983, 102, and in *New Fame, New Love* (xi/1), 82.

Introduction

JULIAN MITCHELL

I

'BUGGERY was invented to fill that awkward hour between even-song and cocktails.' Remarks like that, even today, are challenging as well as funny, and Maurice Bowra's habitual posture was deliberately confrontational. But there was usually a moral purpose behind the preposterousness and wit. 'If the repeated minor shocks of this volcano took many forms,' wrote Anthony Powell, 'their earliest, most essential, was a sense of release.' Bowra, 'so far from attempting to expound tedious moral values of an old-fashioned kind, openly praised the worship of Pleasure'.[1] The satires gathered here were undoubtedly meant to give pleasure; though not always to their subjects.

Cecil Maurice Bowra was born at 3 pm on Good Friday, 8 April 1898, but the auspicious timing did not make him a very ardent Christian. Perhaps the place was unpropitious. It was Kiukiang on the river Yangtze, where his father was a senior official in the Chinese Customs Service. Having survived a move to Manchuria, and a brief evacuation to Japan during the Boxer Rebellion, Maurice first came to England with his parents when he was five. When they returned to China, they left him and his elder brother Edward in the care of their Bowra grandmother in Putney. Her father was a natural son of the Marquess Cornwallis who lost the battle of Yorktown – allowing Maurice to claim in later life that his family was responsible for American independence.

After day school in London and a trip back to China to see his parents and new sister, Maurice was sent, with his brother Edward, to Cheltenham, then regarded as a top college for aspiring army officers. Edward went straight into the senior school, and was to make a successful career in the Royal Engineers, retiring as a Brigadier. But Maurice, in the junior, felt completely out of it,

---

[1] Anthony Powell, *To Keep the Ball Rolling*, vol. 1, *Infants of the Spring*, 1976, 179.

'abandoned by God and man', as he put it in his *Memories*.[1] He didn't know or understand the complex rituals of English boarding-school life, and was at first both miserable and shunned. Though he seemed in adult life a man of enormous self-confidence, this was a 'brassy face' which, however convincing to others, never persuaded Maurice himself.[2] He always claimed he had one skin too few, and the ostracism at Cheltenham made him very unhappy. Schoolboys, however, 'will forgive anything for a joke',[3] and, like so many before and after him, Maurice turned himself into a comedian in order to win, if not the affection, at least the respect of his fellows. He made himself accepted by 'imitating the masters or inventing fantasies about their private lives',[4] and it is in these imaginative efforts to make himself popular that must lie the origins of the wild satirical fantasies of *New Bats in Old Belfries*.

None of his schoolboy verse survives except a long poem, provisionally dated 1913, and called 'Mecanophilus'. It is a rhapsody in double-octosyllabic couplets on the moral benefits that steam-power was bringing to the world. Steam was able

> To pick the weak out of the mire of servile labour and greed,
> To stir up a noble desire where cankers of selfishness feed;
> To teach to the slothful races the lessons of duty and toil,
> The strong love which honour embraces, the courage defeat
> cannot spoil.

The multitudes 'bind up the spirit of steam in an intricate prison of steel' as they approach 'the dawning of freedom's day'. With his knowledge of China, Maurice is able to assure us that progress is proceeding in the East 'along the same roads as the West'.

> Now nation to nation is drawing in hope of more peaceful days,
> The ice of their selfishness thawing 'neath civilisation's rays.

'Mecanophilus' was perhaps an entry for a school poetry prize,

---

[1] *Memories: 1898–1939* [hereafter *Memories*], 1966, 26.
[2] ibid., 124: 'I was not nearly so sure of myself as I should have liked, and this made me present a brassy face to the world and pretend to be more hard-boiled than I was.'
[3] ibid., 28.
[4] ibid.

which explains its hearty imperialist tone, but if so it did not win. Maurice did however win the prize for Latin Verse in 1914, and many other prizes, too, on his way to the top scholarship to New College, Oxford, in 1916. Once his early miseries were over he seems to have been happy enough, and he remained loyal to his old school throughout his life. But 'Mecanophilus' must have been the last wholly optimistic thing Maurice ever wrote.

His brother was already in the army and had seen action by the time Maurice left Cheltenham. Having some months to wait before his call-up, Maurice used the time to go to China for a final visit, spending a month in St Petersburg, or Petrograd as it then was, on the way back, just before the Revolution. There were long queues for food patrolled by whip-cracking Cossacks, and a strong sense of a regime on the verge of collapse. But the Hermitage Museum was open, Chaliapin was singing at the opera, Chekhov was being acted and, most important for Maurice, it may have been then that he first came across the poems of Alexander Blok, of which he was to be a passionate advocate, though not (according to Isaiah Berlin)[1] a very accurate translator. There was also the beautiful sister of a young Guards officer with whom, Maurice wrote, he was obsessed and enraptured. They passed most evenings together and she 'did not bother to talk about her soul or even about mine'.[2] He does not tell us her name, but says both she and he loved her brother. There are two love poems preserved from 1916, not included in this volume, and of wholly conventional form and vocabulary, which may indicate that his rapture was conventional too.

New Bats in Old Belfries is a collection of satires on friends and enemies, written between the 1920s and 1965, put together by Maurice himself some time before his death in 1972 and given to John Sparrow, Warden of All Souls, close friend, literary executor, and subject of some of the most wounding satires. Maurice's other poems are generally of low quality. While they reveal the sensitive thin-skinned inner man, they also show he had no original gift for verse. Just as people found his published scholarly works disappointingly dull compared to his brilliant conversation, so his love poems are disappointingly conventional and lacking in the verbal

---

[1] Letter from Isaiah Berlin to Noel Annan, 31 August 1973, Oxford, Bodleian Library, MS. Berlin 241, fos 128–33, at fo. 131.
[2] *Memories*, 68.

sparkle and wit of the satires. Some of these poems are discussed below, and the most imaginative, if bewildering – 'The wagtail waddles up the grass' – is included in the appendix. Maurice's true poetic talent, and it was prodigious, was for inventive parody.

On his return home from Petrograd there was a further delay before he was called up at the beginning of 1917. Then he was sent to an officer cadet school in, surprisingly, Bloomsbury. Here, and at Lords Cricket Ground and on Salisbury Plain, Maurice suffered the usual humiliations and indignities from sergeant-majors before being commissioned as a second lieutenant. Small and solidly stoutish even when young, he particularly disliked being called 'Shorty'.[1] Among his fellows, however, were three 'magnificently outspoken'[2] Australians who had seen some action and were full of a shocking gaiety and an exciting disrespect for the system. Maurice responded to their irreverence with glee, finding their contempt for pomposity and humbug as liberating from conventional English attitudes as his own was to be for so many Oxford undergraduates in the 1920s.

On Edward's advice he had joined the artillery, and in September 1917 he was sent to join a battery near St Omer. The third battle of Ypres was about to start, and, like the previous battles, at once to become bogged down in appalling mud. Maurice always spoke with revulsion about the conditions in which the troops were expected to fight, and the Dantean visions of hell which can be found in both poems and satires must derive from his personal experience of the front. But he was never a pacifist, and seems to have accepted that the war, once started, had to be carried on, though he never felt any personal animosity towards the Germans. There were many extremely unpleasant moments – for a few minutes he was actually buried alive – and he kept his contempt for the high command and its wilful ignorance of the realities of the war for the rest of his life. But he also kept a sense of humour. Asked to shell the gothic cathedral of Noyon, which the Germans were using as an observation-point, he had, he tells us, qualms, till he remembered that Noyon was the original home of John Calvin, and 'nothing could be too bad, even after four

[1] Reported by Stuart Hampshire to Michael Davie, who records this in chapter 3 of his incomplete draft of a biography of Bowra, fo. 6. See also *Memories*, 72–3.
[2] *Memories*, 75.

centuries, for this enemy of the human race'.[1] To kill the killjoys was always one of the main objects of his life.

His experience of the trenches led Maurice to write a violent and revolutionary poem about the war and the society which produced it which seems never to have been completed to his satisfaction. It is untitled, and from the typescripts seems often to have been revised. It is not clear when it was begun, but it seems heavily influenced by Alexander Blok and T. S. Eliot. Blok's *The Twelve*, which Maurice later translated, was published in 1921, *The Waste Land* in 1922, though Maurice had bought *Prufrock and Other Observations*, along with Hardy's *Moments of Vision* and Yeats's *The Wild Swans at Coole*, while on leave from France, and he may, as I have suggested, have discovered Blok's pre-revolutionary poems in Petrograd in 1916. The poem begins with the description of a decadent casino world obsessed with money and sex:

> Pallid as lard damp faces gaze
> Fixt on illuminated baize.

It then switches abruptly to a horrifying vision of the battlefield after the battle:

> – Bell-beat of wild duck overhead –
> Vultures wheeling to pick the dead.
>
> A pile of peat to feed a fire –
> Carcasses pinned on a shell-shot wire.
>
> Siesta on a sunny mound –
> Gas crawling over blood-drenched ground.
>
> Parapets stacked with mouldy dead
> To keep the wine in the wine-glass red.
>
> Boys bayoneted in the night
> To keep official buttons bright.
>
> Fields sliced to shreds and cities sacked
> To keep a mothy creed intact.

[1] ibid., 83.

> Lithe bodies full of sap shot down
> To gild the glory on a crown.

> To slaughter-pits the victims go,
> Gorging a ghostly triumph-show.

In the next section revenge is called for:

> A king sits in a golden crown –
> Pull the man down, pull the man down [. . .]

> A sleek financier clothed in fur –
> Hang him for a murderer

> [. . .]

> Schoolmasters who trade in lies,
> Tongueless try to moralise.

Then comes a second vision of the battlefield, this time as a frozen cemetery, with the corpses still unburied, and children wandering among them crying for bread. Later the optimism of 'Mecanophilus', where man was in charge of machine, is brutally altered to:

> And ant-like multitudes obey
> Machinery's monarchic sway.

An old woman cries 'Where are the sons I gave to build Paradise?'

This poem is unlike any other in the Bowra canon, and though it has obvious similarities with work by poets such as Owen, Graves and Sassoon, Maurice does not seem to have had any connection with them. (Graves was an Oxford contemporary, at St John's, but he is not mentioned in *Memories*; too hearty, perhaps.) Similar violent revulsion can be found in the satires, but about sex rather than society; there is no repetition of the demand for political change. It was a paradox of Maurice's nature that the deep hatred he felt for brutality could often be brutally expressed – he once told a Fascist he looked forward to drinking out of his skull – and some people found his conversational style bullying as well as booming, with its forceful language and total refusal to utter conventional pieties. But though he says that he and his friends at New College endlessly talked politics, and he was always a man of the left, he was never of the far left, never a revolutionary.

The other side of Maurice, the side he kept secret, is revealed in a few poems he wrote after going up to New College in 1919. The first, dated 1921, about a friend killed in the war, is highly derivative from A. E. Housman. This is the last of the three verses:

> The spring returned and made carouse
> On shattered earth and withered tree;
> But birdless were the broken boughs
> And all the world was dumb to me.

From 1922 is 'Workers', in the style and rhythm of Yeats's 'An Irish Airman Foresees His Death'. It is political in a general rather than a particular way, again describing a world where machines are dominating man, instead of the other way around:

> We get no gain beyond our task,
> We work for an obscurer thing.
> We never seek reward or ask
> For respite or for ransoming.

Also from 1922, his last year as an undergraduate, are two rather wan love poems. To whom they were addressed is not known.

Oxford, like Cheltenham, had begun badly. Maurice had not got on with his philosophy tutor, H. W. B. Joseph, and had had to fight to be allowed to do Mods – perhaps one reason why he later looked so benignly on Wadham undergraduates who wanted to change their courses. But once he was doing what he wanted, Maurice flourished, taking a First in Mods in 1920. Among his tutors was Gilbert Murray, later to be parodied in the satires, and among the undergraduate friends he was also to satirise were Cyril Radcliffe, Roy Harrod, Robert Boothby and Edward Sackville-West. Parody was in the post-war air. Maurice and Radcliffe invented quotations from an imaginary Greek historian called Aristomenes of Tauromenium, successfully fooling their tutor, and he and a group of New College friends wrote poems in what they hoped was the most modern manner:

> Oh buttercups have buttocks
> And so have daffodils

went one of these effusions. 'If we were not creative writers ourselves,' Maurice wrote more than forty years later, 'we were sufficiently interested in such writing to be able to make fun of it.'[1] Half the pleasure of the satires comes from the cleverness of the poetic parodies, though it is easy to overlook this in the delight of their often scabrous fantasy. Sometimes the imitation is of a particular poem; sometimes of the general style of an author; sometimes of a genre. Maurice played lewd variations on poetic tunes familiar to his generation from *Struwwelpeter* to *The Waste Land.*

Once he had taken his Finals, Maurice became a Fellow of Wadham and its Dean. It is then that the satires begin and other forms of poetry tail off, though there is a handful of love poems from 1927 and 1928, perhaps about his unrequited feelings for Pierce Synott, an eccentric Irishman who rose to an important post in the Admiralty. When Maurice put his arm round him he was asked to take it away, and that seems to have been that. None is worth quoting.[2]

II

The 1920s was the decade in which Maurice Bowra's Oxford reputation was made. All the cleverest undergraduates flocked to lunch and dinner in his white-panelled rooms in Wadham: Kenneth Clark, Cyril Connolly, John Betjeman, Hugh Gaitskell, Anthony Powell, Osbert Lancaster, Cecil Day Lewis, Rex Warner, Evelyn Waugh, Henry Yorke (the novelist Henry Green), John Sparrow, Sylvester Gates and (the only woman, as she proudly confessed) Elizabeth Harman, later Pakenham (and eventually Longford). There were one or two young dons, too, notably Lord David Cecil, also at Wadham. Many of Maurice's favoured guests were to leave descriptions of the sparkle and gaiety of the parties he gave on Staircase IV. He was still young, but just that much older than his acolytes, which gave him the chance to dominate. He had been in the war and seen much more of life, in China, Russia and France, than they had. When he held forth, they listened, not

[1] ibid., 114.
[2] One rather more cheerful and two equally dispirited love poems, all undated, are among John Sparrow's papers in the Codrington Library at All Souls (Sparrow Papers Box 57), where there is also a non-satirical epithalamion for Adèle and Howard Hugo dated Valentine's Day 1949. (Howard Hugo, a specialist in comparative literature, was teaching at Harvard during Bowra's visit there in 1948–9.) This last has certain stylistic similarities to 'The wagtail waddles up the grass' (in the appendix, p. 156 below).

respectfully, but with delight at his denunciations of establishment figures – 'shit of hell' and (subtler and more deadly) 'a very able man', and so on. Almost everyone refers to the liberating effect he had on them. Perhaps the best description of the parties is John Betjeman's, and it is appropriately in verse:

> Dinner with Maurice Bowra sharp at eight –
> High up in Wadham's hospitable quad:
> The Gilbert Spencers and the Campbell Gray
> Bright in the inner room; the brown and green
> Of rows and rows of Greek and Latin texts;
> The learning lightly worn; the grand contempt
> For pedants, traitors and pretentiousness.
> A dozen oysters and a dryish hock;
> Claret and *tournedos*; a *bombe surprise* . . .
> The fusillade of phrases ('I'm a man
> More dined against than dining') rattled out
> In that incisive voice and chucked away
> To be re-used in envious common-rooms
> By imitation Maurices [. . .]
> True values there were handed on a plate
> As easily as sprouts and aubergines [. . .]
> And as the evening mellowed into port,
> He read us poems. There I learned to love
> That lord of landscape, Alfred Tennyson;
> Here first heard Thomas Hardy's poetry,
> Master of metre, local as his lanes,
> The one expressive village fatalist.
> Yeats he would chant in deep sonórous voice;
> Bring Rudyard Kipling – then so out of date –
> To his full stature; show that wisdom was
> Not memory-tests (as I had long supposed),
> Not 'first-class brains' and swotting for exams,
> But humble love for what we sought and knew.[1]

Tennyson, Hardy, Yeats, Kipling; the only name missing from this list of favourite poets is Eliot, against whose all-pervading influence Betjeman was then reacting.[2] He added to his poetic praise in prose, writing of Maurice's 'untiring energy, kindness and

[1] John Betjeman, *Summoned by Bells*, 1960, 101–3.
[2] Bevis Hillier, *Young Betjeman*, 1988, 62.

humour'[1] and saying : 'His most endearing quality was his power to build one up in one's own estimation. He did this by listening and either agreeing or suggesting a similar train of thought. In the same way he took one's own troubles on his shoulders.'[2] The relationship with Betjeman remained deep and affectionate, though not uncritical, throughout Maurice's life, and the best and most simply amusing of Maurice's poems are about him and his wife Penelope. Maurice parodies not only Betjeman's life but his style; even the title he gave his collected satires is borrowed from him – unless, that is, Betjeman borrowed it from Maurice.[3] Perhaps it was a shared joke. Betjeman himself was extremely clever at poetic games, and could write a parody of an Oxford lecture (by T. S. R. Boase, himself a subject of Maurice's contempt) even while it was going on. Though Maurice had already started writing satires before Betjeman came up to Oxford, each clearly recognised a fellow-spirit. But there was more than just shared jokes. Maurice genuinely admired Betjeman's serious poetry, even envied it perhaps. Towards the end of his life he wrote him this very warm appreciation:

When I think how few of our friends have fulfilled their first promise and how little one has oneself done from first hopes, your achievement in poetry stands up solid and splendid and encouraging and defiant [. . .] Your poetry is of course entirely your own [. . .] but is also the poetry of our times [. . .] I have always loved your poetry, and it means a great deal to me. I am now old enough to be able to say so.[4]

Maurice never found it easy to say what he truly felt.

'Within those rooms', Betjeman wrote, 'I met my friends for life',[5] and it was there perhaps that Maurice invented his concept of 'our age', so often misinterpreted. Noel Annan used the phrase for the title of a book about the 1920s generation;[6] Isaiah Berlin

---

[1] *Letters*, vol. 1 (xi/1), 79.

[2] *Celebration*, 88.

[3] Betjeman's *New Bats in Old Belfries*, dedicated to 'the Warden, in memory of Nicholas and Dorothy Wadham', was published in 1945. An earlier collection of his poems entitled *Old Lights for New Chancels: Verses Topographical and Amatory* had appeared in 1940.

[4] John Betjeman, *Letters*, vol. 2, *1951 to 1984*, 1995, 309. Maurice's letter was written in October 1966.

[5] *Summoned by Bells* (xxv/1), 102.

[6] *Our Age: Portrait of a Generation*, 1990.

said it referred to people between thirty and seventy;[1] but Maurice, in my experience, used it to describe anyone who was sympathetic to his ideas and attitudes, whether they were nineteen or ninety. It embraced them all.

That Maurice was a great liberator is repeated again and again. For Isaiah Berlin he was 'a major liberating force: the free range of his talk about art, personalities, poetry, civilisations, private life, his disregard of accepted rules, his passionate praise of friends and unbridled denunciation of enemies, produced an intoxicating effect'.[2] Noel Annan said he 'liberated successive years of undergraduates [. . .] The power of his personality, his overwhelming voice and his lightning play with words dominated those who gathered in his rooms.'[3] That he did dominate is undeniable, 'Occasionally shouting out the truth / In forceful nineteen-fourteen army slang'.[4] For Kenneth Clark he became more and more like Dr Johnson as he grew older but his audacity was – again – liberating, and beneath the bombast were real moral values.[5] Cyril Connolly, with whom Maurice later quarrelled, found his ruthless sincerity much preferable to his rival 'Sligger' Urquhart's lack of frankness. Connolly thought Maurice was not the egoist he seemed, though he did create an atmosphere of overpowering intrigue and intensity.[6] Certainly he demanded loyalty from his friends in his many battles with the University's shits of hell. Cecil Day Lewis, a Wadham man, admired 'the urbane effrontery of his manner',[7] though, like some others, he sometimes found him overwhelming and best taken, like strychnine, in small doses.[8] Anthony Powell agreed: 'It was preferable to know Bowra for a time, then get away; returning in due course to appreciate the many things he had to offer.'[9] What is universally agreed is that

[1] loc. cit (xix/1), fo. 128.

[2] Isaiah Berlin, 'Maurice Bowra', in *Personal Impressions*, ed. Henry Hardy, 2nd ed., 1998, 156.

[3] *Our Age* (xxvi/6), 129.

[4] *Summoned by Bells* (xxv/1), 102.

[5] Kenneth Clark, *Another Part of the Wood*, 1974, 93–4.

[6] Cyril Connolly, *A Romantic Friendship: The Letters of Cyril Connolly to Noel Blakiston*, 1975, 78, 72, 56.

[7] C. Day Lewis [who for much of his life did not use the family hyphen], *The Buried Day*, 1960, 164.

[8] Sean Day-Lewis, *C. Day-Lewis: An English Literary Life*, 1980, 251.

[9] *To Keep the Ball Rolling* (xvii/1), 185.

Maurice Bowra opened the world up, where so many closed it down, and discussed openly what many thought better not discussed at all.

One of those things, though never, I imagine, discussed in front of him, was the question of his sexuality. Before introducing Elizabeth Harman, Hugh Gaitskell examined her on her attitude to homosexuality. Once she said it was all right by her, she was allowed to meet him. Later she went out a lot with David Cecil, and they always ended up talking about Maurice: 'Was he a homosexual or not? Was his genius for talk as great as Oscar Wilde's? Was he a committed academic or would he some day enter the world outside Oxford?'[1] Most people assumed that Maurice was, in fact, queer (the word 'gay' did not acquire its current meaning in Britain till the 1960s). John Lowe, the biographer of John Sparrow, describes Sparrow's friendship with Maurice as homosexual but says 'to call them "lovers" might put a modern gloss on a more old-fashioned kind of relationship'.[2] In later years Sparrow made no secret of his affairs with attractive male undergraduates, preferably Old Wykehamists, and he is mocked in several of the satires for his predatory sexuality. Maurice was certainly not predatory. There was no question of undergraduates having to tussle with him in a punt, as Henry Yorke had to tussle with Nevill Coghill.[3] It has been suggested that Adrian Bishop, the subject of 'Old Croaker', with whom Maurice spent much time in Germany and Greece during his sabbatical in 1932, sometimes cruising the queer bars, and about whom he wrote at length in *Memories*, was a lover as well as a friend. Maurice seems to have regarded Bishop as a more powerful version of himself: 'He regarded most orthodox opinion as a conspiracy against enjoyment conducted by Philistines and Pharisees.'[4] But there is, as far as I know, no evidence that Maurice ever went to bed with him or anyone else. Isaiah Berlin said Maurice suffered from 'terror of the blackmailer at the door',[5] which implies there was something to be blackmailed

---

[1] *The Pebbled Shore* (xi/1), 64.

[2] John Lowe, *The Warden: A Portrait of John Sparrow*, 1998, 51.

[3] Jeremy Treglown, *Romancing: The Life and Work of Henry Green*, 2000, 57.

[4] *Memories*, 275.

[5] loc. cit. (xix/1), fo. 131.

about. But he may have wished his friends to think there was when there wasn't.

With his self-consciousness about his size and looks, and with that skin too few, he did not, I imagine, have much sexual self-confidence, and he was always deeply pained by any form of rejection. If, perhaps, there was an underlying fear of women which pushed him towards being homosexual, he was not exclusively so. Noel Annan described him as 'an immensely masculine bisexual',[1] which may be about right. For all the prevailing homosexual atmosphere of his circle, Maurice did ask at least two women to marry him. The first was Elizabeth Harman, who had a number of tête-à-tête lunches with him, at one of which, after a discussion of his recent edition of Pindar's *Pythian Odes*, he suddenly proposed. It's true that it never occurred to her to say yes, but his interest in women did not come altogether as a surprise to her; he had rather annoyed her with his praise of a girl he had met in Ireland. Neither she nor Maurice ever mentioned the subject again, but significantly she felt that, though she was overjoyed at the compliment and felt supremely flattered, Maurice had been wounded by her refusal.[2]

By the time of this proposal Maurice was thirty, had established no lasting emotional relationship with anyone of either sex, and was, perhaps, tiring of impressing undergraduates. His 1927 love poems reveal despair at his situation, he is 'Out of touch, out of mind.' Cyril Connolly wrote that Maurice's genius 'demanded an inner privacy which would never have tolerated the wear and tear of proximity',[3] and this may well have been true. But it would not have stopped him feeling, at times, extremely lonely. It was this loneliness which seems to have led to his second known proposal, in the summer of 1937, to the lesbian Audrey Beecham, niece of the conductor Sir Thomas. The *mariage de convenance* was a well-established convention for homosexuals of both sexes, of course: it provided socially acceptable 'cover'. But dons hardly needed that at Oxford, where homoeroticism among young men coming straight from single-sex schools was taken pretty much for granted, and though Maurice explained his choice with the celebrated remark

[1] *Celebration*, 74.
[2] *The Pebbled Shore* (xi/1), 70–1.
[3] *Celebration*, 46.

that buggers can't be choosers, Isaiah Berlin wrote to Felix Frankfurter that 'He really passionately wants to have a wife, he cannot bear his sexless existence any longer.'[1] Miss Beecham accepted, but soon found the engagement bewildering. She said she felt she was whirling on a roundabout; Bob Boothby advised her to get off, and she did.

Maurice is believed to have made serious advances to several other women, among them Ann Fleming (who figures in 'Apotheosis'), wife successively of Lord O'Neill, killed in the war, Lord Rothermere and Ian Fleming. Maurice told me in the 1950s that she was the only woman to whom he had ever gone down on his knees to beg her to marry him. Mrs Fleming's daughter thinks this a most unlikely story, but I don't know why Maurice should have made it up. It was after dinner, it's true, but he seemed to have tears in his eyes. Isaiah Berlin said Maurice adored her to his dying day, though she may not have adored him. Berlin thought Joan Eyres Monsell was the greatest single love of Maurice's life, of either sex. She was engaged for a time to Alan Pryce-Jones before marrying first John Rayner, and later Patrick Leigh Fermor. Berlin also named Barbara Hutchinson as one of Maurice's loves. She was wife first to Victor Rothschild, then to Rex Warner, then to Niko Ghika. She appears in 'Russian Cradle-Song'.

Some people feel that though he listed many women among his friends in *Memories*, he was often actively and unpleasantly misogynistic in his writings, and there are passages in the satires which make this difficult to deny. The university, with its gross imbalance between the sexes, was decidedly misogynistic at the time, and here Maurice does seem for once to have followed convention. Then, though most of the earlier satires show an unguarded enthusiasm for sex in all its forms, the later are full of an increasing disgust, a positive relish in the fact, to quote his favourite Yeats, that love has built his mansion in the place of excrement. There is a long literary tradition of distaste for the physicality of human love, and sometimes Maurice's characters seem to be ploughing their way through mud and shit, like those of Samuel Beckett, whose own visions of filth derive from Dante's

[1] Letter of 23 August 1937, *Flourishing: Letters 1928–1946*, ed. Henry Hardy, 2004, 251.

Inferno.[1] Readers should take heed; there are funny and affectionate poems in *New Bats in Old Belfries*, but there are others where the *saeva indignatio* is crudely scatological. The most extreme of these, about Richard Crossman, Maurice did not include in the collection, though he didn't destroy it; it may be found, or ignored, in the appendix.

In 1932, after ten years at Wadham, during which, let us not forget, as well as giving lunches and dinners, he had begun to publish books on classical literature, as well as teach it (he was a 'galvanising' teacher, according to Day Lewis), Maurice took his six months' sabbatical. When he returned to Oxford, though lunches and dinners continued, and his reputation remained formidable, things changed. He was no longer the 'unchallenged focal point' for the aesthetes, because the aesthetes had gone down. Oxford, and Maurice himself, were becoming more political. It was no longer Betjeman and Waugh, it was Auden and Spender, and Maurice was never the dominant figure to the new generation that he had been to the old. Nor did he ever 'enter the world outside Oxford', he stayed inside and became a university politician, Warden of Wadham for thirty-two years and a notable Vice-Chancellor. The wit, the energy, the outrageousness, the often overlooked kindness, the powerful personality remained, but they were exercised on his contemporaries now more than on the young. What did remain unchanged, was indeed perhaps sharpened, was his pleasure in mocking them.

III

New Bats in Old Belfries contains all the satires Maurice is known to have written, except those poems and stanzas omitted for reasons explained in the editorial preface; but there may be others which have still to come to light. Most are given a date, and I am assuming in what follows, perhaps not always correctly, that the date is that of writing rather than of later revision. In Maurice's lifetime the poems were only ever 'privately circulated', but they were often also literally 'party pieces' which he read to select friends after dinner at Wadham:

---

[1] Maurice wrote a preface to Beckett's translation of Octavio Paz's *Anthology of Mexican Poetry* (1958).

Having taken down from its locked shelf the famous manuscript volume, on which no eye but the poet's had ever been allowed to rest, [Maurice] would settle himself in his chair, raise a hand for silence and begin the reading. First would come a selection of the old favourites – 'The Ballad of Bob Boothby' in the manner of Thomas Hardy, perhaps, or the 'Ode to Penelope Betjeman' – and then, if we were lucky, would follow the premiere of a new and recently completed composition. This would be rendered in deeper and even more impressive tones, the subtleties and more lyrical passages emphasised by monitory finger-wagging or free and sweeping gestures of the hand. At the end he would turn interrogatively to the company, '*Rather* beautiful, don't you think?'[1]

Apart from such readings, just how private was the circulation? Isaiah Berlin claimed 'Maurice was, all his life, *terrified* of his poems falling into the hands of anyone outside the charmed circle',[2] and the basic audience must have been no wider than the group of old friends and enemies satirised. But the former often copied and passed the poems around, and their existence was no secret. We know that John Betjeman was sent the early genial poems about himself, though whether Maurice sent him the more vicious 'Prize Song' of 1959 we don't. Were the victims of the satire always directly informed? Surely not those most venomously lampooned, though, life being what it is, they must soon have found out from 'friends' concerned for their reputation. People have always enjoyed squibs of this sort – I spent several years of my life attempting to edit those from the reigns of James I and Charles I. Though they were more political than Maurice's, their anonymous authors shared his delight in gossip, insinuation and accusations of sexual malpractice, and the poems were widely distributed.

Maurice's too were better known than one might think. In June 1954 Stephen Spender and Alan Pryce-Jones were treated to a reading in All Souls by John Sparrow which went on till two in the morning. '[The poems] showed a genius which I would not have suspected for M[aurice], dazzling as he is,' wrote Spender. 'That someone in his position should have written these poems, that they should be circulated and read by his friends, that he should have

---

[1] Osbert Lancaster, in *Celebration*, 108. For his account of a recitation of the prothalamium for Kenneth Clark during an air raid, see 13/§.

[2] loc. cit (xix/1), fo. 130.

given them to the wife of the editor of a great newspaper, and that they should actually be known to members of the cabinet, is amazing.'[1] No doubt it was Sparrow who enlightened the cabinet ministers, of whom All Souls could usually boast a few. The newspaper editor was Michael Berry, created Lord Hartwell in 1968, Chairman and Editor-in-Chief of the *Daily Telegraph*. His wife was Pamela, daughter of F. E. Smith, Wadham's celebrated legal alumnus. At Oxford in the 1950s there was a rumour that Maurice had written a poem about her which, either by oversight or with malice aforethought, probably the latter, he left in the lavatory when she came to dinner. She found it and was satisfactorily shocked. Alas, no such poem seems to exist, and Spender's story suggests she was in fact another recipient of some, if not all, of the satires. But the possibility of starring in one of Maurice's poems must have contributed to the caution with which so many people treated him.

The only person to have written anything about the satires (and to have published long fragments) is Noel Annan.[2] 'Whether or not he [Maurice] was released in his verse from his inhibitions, it is certainly unsurpassable in the vigour, candour and fantasy with which it describes sexual activity [...] The heterosexual verse is usually of a singular savagery and invention, paeans to the goddesses of fertility, lust and potency.' (Annan may have been thinking particularly of 'Heldengesang', the prothalamium Maurice wrote for him. It is very much more savage than the one he wrote for Kenneth Clark.) Annan went on: 'He did not view all the activities of the Homintern [a term of Maurice's invention] with benign equanimity. Someone as masculine as he had little patience with old sissies [...].'

The earliest poems were written when Maurice was still an undergraduate, and the very first, or the one he chose to place first, is based on Arthur Hugh Clough's 'The Latest Decalogue' ('Thou shalt not kill, but needst not strive / Officiously to keep alive'). The eminent classical epigraphist Marcus Niebuhr Tod is imagined finding an alternative Decalogue, dated 1698 BC, in Sinai. Significantly the fragments of stone indicate a thoroughly liberal, indeed

---

[1] Stephen Spender, *Journals, 1939–1983*, ed. John Goldsmith, 1985, 155.
[2] *Celebration*, 76–81; see also xi/1 above.

immoral, God, who urges human beings to do pretty much everything they like. Not altogether unlike Maurice himself, he goes much farther in freeing human beings from all moral inhibitions. Also from undergraduate days is a parody of T. S. Eliot's 'A Cooking Egg' with a dig at Sylvester Gates, the New College friend who became a banker and appears in later satires. After these two poems, Maurice is Dean of Wadham and writing character sketches of the Warden, Joseph Wells, and the Headmaster of Uppingham, the Revd R. H. Owen, and three distinctly irreligious 'Confirmation Songs'.

Unless we are scholars of the period, we are not likely to find these early squibs very funny, though the poem about Tod, an imitation of a parody, is clever enough. It is with the 'Prothalamium' for Kenneth Clark of 1927 that we can begin to share the joke. It is an insinuating farewell from the homosexual world ('Other loves who love him yet') to someone who has escaped, or grown up, into the heterosexual. The Clarks, if they read the poem, and I assume they did, don't seem to have been in the least offended. They remained close friends of both Maurice and John Sparrow, who, the poem implies, was one of Kenneth's ex-lovers. They invited Sparrow to be godfather to their daughter, and had Maurice as a regular Christmas guest at Saltwood Castle, where the only difficulty was in providing him, in old age, with the constant audience he craved.[1] That same year Maurice wrote a sort of farewell to his undergraduate friends, Cyril Connolly among them ('Well versed in ancient insincerity'). It is a parody of Yeats's 'In Memory of Major Robert Gregory', from *The Wild Swans at Coole* – one of the books Maurice bought while on leave from the front. Both these poems are full of his wild exaggeration, which becomes even wilder as time goes on. Maurice is not describing, he is fantasising for entertainment; the suggestions and insinuations are never to be taken literally.

There is then a gap of ten years before 'The Late Lorn Lesbian' and 'Uffington Downs'. 'Uffington Downs' is a wonderfully inventive parody of Tennyson's *Idylls of the King*, and many will find it the most enjoyable of the satires, because so obviously

---

[1] The Annans also found him a difficult Christmas guest towards the end of his life; he was not good with children. (Personal communication.)

affectionate. The Betjemans, John and Penelope, always brought out the best in Maurice, partly, I suspect, because though he found them funny, he was also very fond of them. In the 1930s they were living at Uffington, under the White Horse, as was, for a time, Adrian Bishop (before he became briefly a monk), and among their neighbours were the Osbert Lancasters. Maurice was a frequent visitor, and Lancaster did the wonderful cartoon of them all singing 'Sumer is icumen in' to astonished locals at a Village Hall concert reproduced as the frontispiece to this volume. No doubt poetry games were played after dinner. 'Uffington Downs' is a very funny fantasy about the Betjemans' imagined sexual innocence, and how this was overcome by observation of the horses of the (wholly imaginary) Pakenham stud, and a bridle and snaffle. Betjeman was sufficiently amused to send a copy to a friend, though he did call Maurice 'that old stinker' and warn that the poem was 'a bit rude'. It seems very mild by modern standards, and makes one wonder if Betjeman wrote poems about Maurice in return; if so, they do not seem to have survived.

The Betjemans continued to be subjects for Maurice's satire, and there are three poems about them from 1940, which, though a catastrophic year for the country, seems to have been one of great inspiration for Maurice. Unfortunately his *Memories* stop in 1939, and he does not tell us what he actually felt during the period between the German invasion of France and the Blitz. We do know, however, that he had witnessed at first hand the horrors of Nazi Germany during his many visits there in the 1930s, and it was probably anger and frustration at not being given a war job which drove him to write so much.

Betjeman had joined the Observer Corps before the war, and was hoping to get into the RAF, but was turned down on medical grounds. One of the 1940 poems is a fantasy about him actually in the RAF and going for a spin to look at 'an eighteenth century rood-loft / And some box-pews in King's Lynn'. Another is about Penelope alone while Betjeman is away, a parody of one of Betjeman's own poems. The third is in the form of an old ballad, about the wedding of Sir John, and though precisely dated 8 August 1940 reads like one of the pre-war Uffington weekend poems written up.

Apart from these there are 1940 satires on the Oxford figures

R. C. Zaehner and Isaiah Berlin (another parody of a Betjeman poem, itself a parody of Thomas Hardy), and the eccentric composer Lord Berners, who lived not far away at Faringdon with Robert Heber-Percy and a flock of pigeons dyed saffron yellow, shocking pink and turquoise blue. Maurice put Berners up for a while when he imagined he was losing his money, and found him war work cataloguing books at the Taylorian. In return Berners put Maurice into his rather feeble 1941 novel, *Far from the Madding War*, as the Provost of an Oxford college who, depressed at not being a man of action, is writing memoirs which 'could [not] be published until after his death, and when they were, [...] would undoubtedly cause a certain amount of surprise and annoyance to a great many grandchildren'.[1] There is also a quatrain on the fall of Lord Reith and rise of Kenneth Clark, in imitation of Hilaire Belloc, and a poem on Harold Nicolson at the Ministry of Information, the only one in which the war gets a mention. 'Air Populaire', on A. J. ('Freddie') Ayer's wife Renée, later the wife of Stuart Hampshire, illustrates all too forcefully Annan's remark about the 'singular savagery and invention' of Maurice's heterosexual verse.

Maurice's creative wartime vein continued, the spring of 1941 bringing a fantasy on John Sparrow's sexual activities in the army and their unusual punishment, but more importantly the long poem 'Old Croaker' on Adrian Bishop. Bishop had come out of his monastery to join Intelligence, and was working in Persia, where he later fell or was pushed to his death down a staircase in Tehran. Annan calls 'Old Croaker' 'a threnody upon his life and on the lives of all the homosexuals in the twenties'.[2] It recalls the nights Maurice spent with Bishop in low dives in Berlin ('Kennen sie Christopher Isherwood?') and Athens, picking up evzones, and covers almost every aspect of pre-war queer life. It is also an elaborate parody of *The Waste Land*, in fact the most sustained and imaginative of all Maurice's parodies. It has so many references it needs rather more notes than *The Waste Land* itself.

After this major effort come poems on Maurice's New College

---

[1] Lord Berners, *Far from the Madding War*, 1941, 69–70. Bowra was still saying in the 1960s that he meant to write a Secret History of his times, on the model of Procopius, to be published only after his death. It could be argued that *New Bats in Old Belfries* is it.

[2] *Celebration*, 78.

friend Cyril Radcliffe, by now an eminent barrister, and a long poem about Sylvester Gates being sent to prison for violent assault, on which John Sparrow noted: 'fiction from beginning to end'. How did Maurice find the time for so much writing? Was it the result of having to stay in Britain for his vacations instead of going abroad? In any case, he was at it again in July 1941, with a very funny poem about the hypochondriac Edward Sackville-West, and Christmas produced a long ballad about Bob Boothby. Between these come a satire on several fellows of All Souls and a piece about Gilbert and Mary Murray, apparently gentle, but in plodding couplets which are a devastating criticism of Murray's translations of classical texts.

Maurice was Professor of Poetry from 1946 to 1951, a role which seems to have temporarily checked his own poetic impulse, though in 1950, the year before he became Vice-Chancellor, there is another sudden rush of poems, mainly about his non-Oxford friends, including Raymond Mortimer and Rosamond Lehmann. One of these is a long parody of Edith Sitwell's *Façade*. The spate continues into 1951 with poems on John Bowle and the election of John Sparrow to the Wardenship of All Souls. Thereafter Oxford excitements are the main subject, though Bob Boothby gets another blast. In 1959 there is an unusually snide poem about John Betjeman, teasing him quite savagely for sucking up to Princess Margaret when she presented him with the 1958 Duff Cooper Prize, for which Maurice was one of the judges. According to Lady Diana Cooper, Betjeman 'was crying and too moved to find an apology for words',[1] so perhaps he deserved it. Maurice did not like America, and Stuart and Renée Hampshire get a going over for deserting to Princeton in 1963 (though Stuart was to return to succeed Maurice as Warden of Wadham). The final two poems, from 1965, are on the continuing row at All Souls about the purpose of the College, in which John Sparrow's negativism triumphed.

The satires cover a period of more than forty years. They are personal, not political, their subject is a small group of friends and enemies; they are malicious, spiteful, back-biting, bitchy, frequently filthy, frequently funny – just the sort of thing, in fact, that the

[1] Philip Ziegler, *Diana Cooper*, 1981, 310.

group enjoyed. They are, though, private jokes, not public ones; they never attempt critical comment on society at large, and in this they can be accused of lacking ambition. The same can be said of Maurice, and he knew it. The question Elizabeth Harman and David Cecil asked – would he some day enter the world outside Oxford? – he answered himself in the letter praising Betjeman's poems: 'When I think how few of our friends have fulfilled their first promise and how little one has oneself done from first hopes [...].' This was not, I believe, false modesty, but his genuine opinion. Behind the Bowra bombast there was always a secret sense of failure, that recurring lack of self-confidence; he had many days of the 'black dog'. If he confined himself largely to Oxford, it was because he felt safe there, he knew how to dominate the other dons, just as he had dominated the undergraduates of the 1920s. London he left mostly alone. (The poems about Bob Boothby are exceptional in being about a politician; they are also among the less successful.)

The satires show the scabrous and venomous side of Maurice, and as he got older they show it more clearly. He became bitterly envious of others' success, he cared too much about public honours; reading the collected satires may make one think their author was a fairly horrible man. But they reveal only a small if highly accomplished part of a very complex character. Maurice knew how to entertain his friends with spite and salaciousness, just as he had entertained his fellow schoolboys with fantasies about the masters, but he was also a famously good head of house, a wonderful Warden of Wadham, who took enormous care over individual students, often without letting anyone know. I cannot end without saying how generous, sympathetic and understanding he was to me personally.[1] I feel about him just as the undergraduates did in the 1920s. I loved the jokes and the fusillades against the 'very able' men, all the vainglorious things for which he was famous; but I shall always be most grateful, as they were, for the way he opened the world up and helped to set me free from the stultifying influences of my conventional upbringing. Maurice's main role in life was not as a classical scholar, not as a satirist, not as an administrator; it was as a liberator. Perhaps it is because I still

[1] See my *A Disgraceful Anomaly*, 2003.

feel so warmly towards him, thirty years after he died, that I think I can detect deeper feeling than at first appears in some of these poems, a wish to do more than simply amuse – as though amusing were easy. Just as Maurice's proposals of marriage may have had devious intent, so may the satires. Here they are, for readers to judge for themselves.

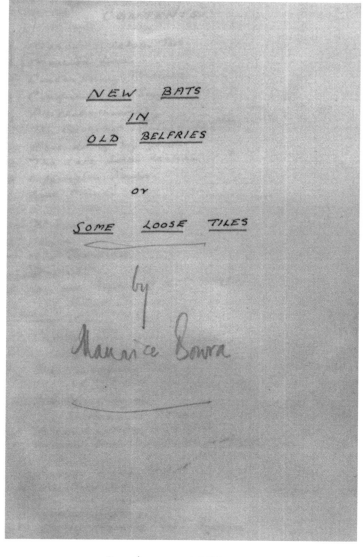

Bowra's manuscript title page:
John Sparrow has added the author's name

Marcus Niebuhr Tod.

I sing of Marcus Niebuhr Tod
Who found the autograph of God.

Carved on a Sinaitic cliff
He found Jehovah's hieroglyph.
A casual glance assured the date
As B.C. 1698.
Convinced that no epigraphist
Had entered it on any list,
The worthy Marcus looked around
And found in fragments on the ground
An interesting Hebrew text
Concerning this world and the next.
With scrupulous and loving care
He joined the pieces lying there,
And with a scholar's zeal restored
Words written by the living Lord:

"Go, worship other gods than me:
I feel the need of company.

"And copy bird or beast or fish
In wood or stone, if that's your wish.

"Rightly or wrongly, take my name:
To me it's very much the same.

"If toil on week-days you must shirk,
Then keep the Sabbath for your work.

The first page of the first poem in Bowra's manuscript,
with a clarification by Sparrow

Marcus Niebuhr Tod

I sing of Marcus Niebuhr Tod[1]
Who found the autograph of God.

Carved on a Sinaitic cliff
He found Jehovah's hieroglyph.
A casual glance assured the date
As BC 1698.
Convinced that no epigraphist
Had entered it on any list,
The worthy Marcus looked around
And found in fragments on the ground
An interesting Hebrew text
Concerning this world and the next.
With scrupulous and loving care
He joined the pieces lying there,
And with a scholar's zeal restored
Words written by the living Lord:

'Go, worship other gods than me:
I feel the need of company.

'And copy bird or beast or fish
In wood or stone, if that's your wish.

---

[1] M. N. Tod (1878–1974), Fellow of Oriel 1903–47, University Reader in Greek Epigraphy 1927–49, was a scholar of international renown and a Presbyterian of deep religious beliefs. In his obituary of Ronald Syme, 'Ronald Syme 1903–1989', *Proceedings of the British Academy* 84 (1993), *1993 Lectures and Memoirs*, 539–63, at 542–4, G. W. Bowersock quotes all but the last 13 lines of this parody of Arthur Hugh Clough's 'The Latest Decalogue' (in *The Poems and Prose Remains of A. H. Clough*, vol 2, *Poems*, 1869), misattributing the poem to Syme. He was understandably misled by the presence in Syme's archive at Wolfson College, Oxford, of a copy of the text, and by the fact that the sentiments expressed in the poem might well be Syme's too. The relationship of the poem to a 6–8-line version current in Oriel College in various forms, and often attributed to Dalziel Llewellyn Hammick of that College, is unclear.

'Rightly or wrongly, take my name:
To me it's very much the same;

'If toil on weekdays you must shirk,
Then keep the Sabbath for your work.

'If what you want's a good long life,
With parents keep continual strife.

'Kill anyone who worries you:
It's easier and safer too.

'And if your neighbour's wife is free,
Of course commit adultery.

'If others have what you have not,
Why not take steps to steal the lot?

'False evidence against a friend
Brings much advantage in the end.

'If someone has what takes your eye,
Ask, and you'll get it by and by.'

These mystic words did Marcus find,
And laid them carefully to mind,
But not before upon his knees
He knelt and took a loving squeeze.
When in the *Epigraphic Year*
The learned saw the work appear,
They pressed the ill-considered view
That here at last was found the true
Editio princeps[1] of the Ten
Commandments given unto men,

---

[1] First edition.

Which Moses cast upon the ground.
This text, they claimed, had Marcus found.
But Marcus did not welcome this
Improbable hypothesis,
And thought that it was far too bold
For any prudent man to hold . . .
Perambulating Oriel Quad
I thought of Marcus Niebuhr Tod.

1920, 1940

Married Love

for T. S. Eliot

Apocalyptic Aguecheek
Makes ithyphallic epigrams,
While Pippit puts between her breasts
A ruby of a million grammes.

A naked Mozambiquer leads
A catawampus on a string;
It climbs the steep ascent to heaven
And searches Pippit's inner ring.

Her husband snores upon his back,
Dreaming of copper-bottomed shares;
The catawampus takes its joy
In unfamiliar shadowy lairs.

I shall not need charity in heaven,
For I shall meet Sylvester Gates.[1]
We two shall in the court of heaven
Indulge in apolaustic hates.

---

§ In 1921 Marie Stopes (1880–1910), like Bowra a liberator, helped to set up the first birth-control clinic in Britain; the title of this poem is also that of her 1918 book celebrating the glories of sex within marriage. However, the poem's form and deliberately obscure vocabulary echo the 1920 collection, *Poems*, by T. S. Eliot (1885–1965) particularly 'The Hippopotamus', the Sweeney poems and 'A Cooking Egg', in which last a girl called Pipit [*sic*] sits near a book entitled *Views of the Oxford Colleges* and the poet claims: 'I shall not want Honour in Heaven / For I shall meet Sir Philip Sidney.'

[1] Sylvester Gates (1901–72), New College classics 1920–4; later barrister and banker; according to John Sparrow's biographer John Lowe 'a man noted for his wisdom' (*The Warden* [xxviii/2], 39); he was described in an obituary as possessing 'a fine mind and a fastidious temper' (*The Times*, 11 November 1972, 18), but see 63/§.

I shall not need chastity in heaven,
For I shall be with Oliver Thynne,[1]
And *alternando*[2] we shall go
In and out and out and in.

1921

---

[1] Oliver Thynne (1901–78), New College history 1920–3; later President, British Federation of Master Printers.

[2] 'Taking turns'.

CONTEMPORARY PORTRAITS

1923

I

Joseph Wells Esq., MA, Warden of Wadham College

Church
And State.
Lots of Church,
But not much State.
I know we said it,
But did we really mean it?
If Christ were alive,
He would like the Empire;
He would be a corporal
In the ASC.[1]
Lord Birkenhead[2] has said it,
That puissant nobleman,
The first Earl of Birkenhead,
Statesman, Churchman,
Englishman,
Wadham man –
God save the King.

---

§ Joseph Wells (1855–1929), Warden of Wadham 1913–27, the imagined speaker, was described by Bowra as 'a man of unusual sweetness and simplicity', who, on breaking a newly-made College resolution, remarked: 'I know we made that rule, but surely we never meant to keep it' (*Memories*, 129).

[1] Army Service Corps.

[2] F(rederick) E. Smith (1872–1930), first Earl of Birkenhead 1921; read law at Wadham then became barrister, academic, author and Conservative politician; Attorney-General 1915–19; Lord Chancellor 1919–22; High Steward of Oxford University 1922.

Revd R. H. Owen, MA,
Headmaster of Uppingham School

Boys will be boys,
Thank God.
The Church of England says so,
And it ought to know.
Roll up the map of Greece;[1]
We shan't need it again
Till Speech Day.
The British Empire stands
On and for
Beef, beer, bacon and eggs,
And rowing,
Stroke, seven, six, five, four, three, two, bow.
Damn the bloody black man.
The Church of England says so,
And it ought to know.[2]

---

§ The speaker is Reginald H. Owen (1887–1961), Headmaster of Uppingham School 1916–34; a rowing blue in 1910 while an undergraduate at Wadham; later (1947–60) Archbishop of New Zealand.

[1] Under the Treaty of Lausanne (1923) Greece lost eastern Thrace to Turkey.

[2] Cf. 'Balliol, Balliol / Bring out your black men / Jack Johnson says so / And he ought to know' from the Gordouli, the Balliol–Trinity taunting chant (*The Encyclopaedia of Oxford*, ed. Christopher Hibbert, 1988, 157).

CONFIRMATION SONGS

I

Christ Church, Woburn Square

I hope some day to say 'Boo'
To a very big goose,[1]
'Boo' though I play fast and loose
And join in the hullaballoo
And am somewhat obtuse.
Yet the Lord, my Lord, offers peace
When the day shall dawn for me too
Which bids me have nothing to do
With the goose, with the geese.

§ The title refers to the church where the profoundly religious Christina Rossetti (1830–84) worshipped for many years. Her poems, many written for children, are characterised by short lines of irregular rhyme and length.

[1] John Sparrow notes that Dr M. J. Rendall, Headmaster of Winchester College, once declared to a pupil, 'I hope that some day you will say "Boo" to a very big goose.'

All Saints' Church, Ludlow

The Bishop, while the organ plays,
　　Dispenses grace divine
On lips God made for other ways
　　Of taking bread and wine.

The Bishop, while the anthems sound,
　　Blesses each bended head,
And scatters upon stony ground
　　The seed they may not shed.

The seed they sow while manhood lasts,
　　The straight, the strong, the bold;
But each for every seed he casts
　　Must reap an hundredfold.

The bread the body craves must be
　　Demanded on their knees;
The wine their eyes should dread to see
　　They drain it to the lees.

---

§ A(lfred) E. Housman (1859–1936), the inspiration for this poem, had close
connections with Ludlow; his ashes are buried beside the wall of the parish
church, dedicated (*pace* this poem's title) to St Laurence.

III

Clevedon Parish Church

I dream that I am young once more
    And kneel before the altar-rail,
    While my loved Arthur glimmers pale
And kneels beside me on the floor.

The kind old bishop speaks of love,
    Of service and of higher things.
    In samite robe a choirboy sings:
He too has thoughts of things above.

The kind old bishop lays his hands
    Upon the head I love to touch:
    I am not jealous overmuch
And mark his person as he stands.

I dally with a world unseen:
    He speaks of all that matters most,
    Of Father and of Holy Ghost,
And duty to our gracious Queen.

§ St Andrew's Church, Clevedon, in Somerset, is the burial-place of Arthur
Henry Hallam (1811–33), close friend of Alfred, Lord Tennyson (1809–92),
whose *In Memoriam AHH* (1850) is the rhythmical model for this poem.

Prothalamium

Angels of St James's Park,[1]
Make the bed for Kenneth Clark:[2]
Make it when such loves are sealed
Broad as any battlefield.
When he strips him for the fight,
Help him in his work tonight.
See that all the night till morn
No preventative is torn;
Many a useless child may live
From a torn preventative.
No more time to flog and frig:
K must dance another jig,
Dance it with his good wife Jane[3]
In and out and in again.
When his legs are flung across,
When his hands are in the moss,

§ Osbert Lancaster describes Bowra giving a rare public performance of this poem: 'One night during the blitz, carried away by port, enthusiasm and the prospect of an air-raid, which he always found particularly stimulating, he recited the whole of the Epithalamion [*sic*] for Kenneth Clark in the middle of Pratt's Club to an audience consisting of Evelyn Waugh, Lord Birkenhead, a handful of puzzled but attentive ensigns from the Brigade of Guards, and myself.' *Celebration*, 108.

[1] The Clarks' first home after their marriage was a service flat in St Ermin's Hotel, near St James's Park.

[2] Cf. 'Matthew, Mark, Luke and John, / Bless the bed that I lie on' (from one version of a traditional prayer for children). Kenneth Clark (1903–83), Baron Clark 1969; Winchester College 1917–22, Trinity College, Oxford, 1922–5; art historian, author and broadcaster; Director of the National Gallery 1934–45. Clark claimed always to have been enthusiastically heterosexual: 'I have never felt the faintest inclination to homosexuality.' *Another Part of the Wood* (xxvii/5), 70.

[3] Elizabeth ('Jane') Martin (1902–76) married Kenneth Clark in January 1927.

Panting heart on panting heart,
Breast to breast and part to part,
Let him in that hour forget
Other loves who love him yet,
Those he asked to let him on,
Horsley[1] and Sparrovian John,[2]
Those who tried to keep him good,
Venables[3] and little Wood.[4]
Come not here to spoil the fun,
Shade of Harold Nicolson,[5]
Come not Kenneth to alarm
In the darkness thick and warm.
Angels, watch behind the scenes
While the greenhorn has his greens.

1927

---

[1] Possibly Rupert Horsley (1905–88), a Wykehamist contemporary of Clark who went on to Brasenose College.

[2] John Sparrow (1906–92), New College 1925–9, a contemporary of Clark at Winchester who became a close friend of his and Bowra's; classicist, barrister, bibliophile and homosexual; later (1952–77) Warden of All Souls.

[3] Peter Venables (1905–69), a friend of Clark's while they were at Winchester; later a Catholic priest.

[4] Not certainly identified.

[5] Harold Nicolson (1886–1968), Balliol 1904–7; diplomat, politician and author. A bisexual with an enthusiastic appetite for male members of his own social class, Nicolson became a close, lifelong friend of Bowra and Sparrow. They both campaigned for him in the 1956 election of the Professor of Poetry, in which Nicolson was defeated by W. H. Auden, and Sparrow used Nicolson's Albany flat as his London base once he became Warden of All Souls.

The Architect to his Lady

No art or craft profanes my verse,[1]
No aspidistras venture near.
Listen in silence.[2] I rehearse
The architecture of my dear.

Polychromatic is each tit;
To them must Keble's glory yield.
Her Early English nipples fit
Like gargoyles carved for Butterfield.[3]

Palladian[4] her fluted thighs
Give shade and warmth to all who come;
But oh! what Inigo could devise
The barrel-vaulting of her bum?

Her navel in the Tuscan taste
Brighton's Pavilion would outshine;

---

§ In 1927 John Betjeman (1906–84), the inspiration for this fantastical poem, was still an undergraduate at Magdalen College, but his passion for architecture was already evident.

[1] In his first article for the *Isis* ('Our Lovely Lodging-Houses', 27 October 1926, 19), Betjeman had bemoaned the usual standard of decoration in student 'digs' – often featuring 'a magnificent aspidistra' – but concluded that a move to the 'arts and crafts' style of decoration advocated by William Morris would, if carried out by an Oxford landlady, produce 'even more horrible vistas'.

[2] An echo of Horace's 'odi profanum vulgus [. . .] favete linguis' ('I hate the uninitiated masses [. . .] favour me with your tongues [i.e. keep silent]'), *Odes* 3. 1.

[3] The designs of William Butterfield (1814–1900), the architect of Keble, were Victorian Gothic in style and often included lavish polychromatic decoration.

[4] Andrea Palladio (1508–80) re-introduced the traditions of classical architecture to Italy. His influence spread to Britain through the designs of Inigo Jones (1573–1652).

On round Egyptian pillars based
Her architrave shines next to mine.

Could Waterhouse or Gilbert Scott[1]
Such curves and rectilinears join,
Or carve so neat a lovers' knot
In the rococo of her groin?

Her quim in neo-Georgian style
Presents the glories of the Strand,
Where, like Bush House's organ pile,[2]
Erect, rectangular I stand.

Could even Batty Langley[3] see
How many orders here there are?
But what are all her styles to me
When I am perpendicular?

20 July 1927

---

[1] Alfred Waterhouse (1830–1905) and Sir George Gilbert Scott (1811–78) were leading architects of the Victorian Gothic revival.

[2] The central portion of Bush House on the Strand, now home of the BBC's World Service, was built in 1923 and is remarkable for its massive columned portico.

[3] Batty Langley (1696–1751), architect and garden designer, who invented five new orders of quasi-Gothic architecture; one of his many instructional books on architecture is entitled *The Builder's Chest-Book; or A Complete Key to the Five Orders of Columns in Architecture* (1727).

Friends of my Youth

Dedicated to W. B. Yeats

Tonight I cannot sleep upon my bed
For those old names that brim up in my head,
New College friends of undergraduate days,
Or maybe friends of K's,[1]
Whose corporal images have wandered far
For petty traffic or the outrageous bar.
Tonight they share my courtesy in this room;
For common learning once was ours,
Or those uncommon paramours,
Though now they all are silent as the tomb.

Hew Anderson[2] comes first. Religious, he
Found beatific bliss in sodomy.
Too conscience-stricken, he was generous
To lovers out at Exeter or the House,[3]
Though once, by a Platonick passion stirred
For Joseph,[4] he achieved a Third:
But later being most dissatisfied
With logical or it may be
Political philosophy
He bought a flat in Bloomsbury and died.

---

§ An imitation of 'In Memory of Major Robert Gregory' by W. B. Yeats
(1865–1939), in *The Wild Swans at Coole*, 1919.

[1] Kenneth Clark was invariably called 'K' by his friends.

[2] Hew Anderson (1900–25), New College classics 1919–22; according to
Bowra, 'essentially an artist [who] insisted that he must first learn philosophy'
(*Memories*, 94).

[3] Christ Church, from its Latin name, 'Aedes Christi', 'the house of Christ'.

[4] H[orace] W. B. Joseph (1867–1943), senior philosophy tutor at New
College 1895–1932. As his tutor, Joseph left Bowra 'totally foiled and
humiliated': Joseph's 'aim was to make his pupils think correctly, and this aim
he pursued with no care for their vanity or self-respect' (*Memories*, 99–100).

Next Walter Wright[1] I call, a Wykehamist,
Who thought it sweetest destiny to be kissed
By his own sex, and never gave a thought
To failures which examinations brought.
An arrogant coal-owner he
Did everything regardlessly,
Till all his caviare and roasted quails
But brought him to a trivial way
When in nightclubs he should pay
Women abandoned by the Prince of Wales.

And then I call on Strauss.[2] When he was born,
The opposing stars had crossed his birth with scorn.
He boasted his descent from Solomon
And Sheba, but the inconsiderate moon
Had crossed him so that all his many years
He nothing knew but fears.
He tried to turn the universe to a joke,
But dithered in a speechless dread
Lest we, for all the words we said,
Might leave him like an old pig in a poke.

Next Radcliffe[3] comes, who little cared for love
And gave it all his thought. None could him move
From counterfeited words or playing a part
In some sham ceremony of the heart;
But hidden he would seek some logic out

---

[1] Edward Fitzwalter Wright (1902–57), from a wealthy family of coal-owners; Winchester College 1915–20 (in the same house as Kenneth Clark); Christ Church 1920–3; later High Sheriff of Derbyshire.

[2] Eric Strauss (1894–1961), wounded in the First World War, New College medicine 1918–21. A Roman Catholic convert of Jewish descent, he was the leader of a group of five friends – the others being Bowra, Hew Anderson, Roy Harrod and Stephen Tomlin – who wrote light-hearted modern poetry (see p. xxiii above); Bowra described him, despite his 'gift for nonsense', as 'a lonely, pathetic figure' who 'almost clamoured for help and affection' (*Memories*, 115). Later an eminent psychologist.

[3] Cyril Radcliffe (1899–1977), 1st Viscount Radcliffe 1962; New College classics 1919–21; barrister, judge and public servant; Lord of Appeal in Ordinary 1949–64.

That he might find a thought
Where wedded to consuming ecstasy
He should achieve for every mood
By logical exactitude
A presence in the Primum Mobile.[1]

And last I number Cyril Connolly,[2]
Well versed in ancient insincerity.
Who fearing that a eunuch's fate was his,
Found reverence in hearing Longden[3] piss.
He played at living in a lordlier age
And made the world his stage,
Till all the learning he had found at school
Monotonous completion brought
To fatten his lascivious thought,
And he could see no further than his tool.

Others come up before the mind's bright eye,
Clamouring to be recognised, but I
Find little pleasure in their coming thus
Unasked, whose ways were ceremonious
When in past time they came to visit me
To drink of cocoa or of tea.
But now that I am old they come to mock
Or with a ghostly insolence
To tear my covering of pretence
And stop my sleep at midnight by the clock.[4]

1927

---

[1] 'First mover'; in ancient and medieval cosmology the outermost, purest
and fastest-moving of the concentric spheres which constituted the universe
and were thought to revolve round the earth; its speed caused the movement
of the inner spheres.

[2] Cyril Connolly (1903–74), Etonian, Balliol history 1922–25; critic, editor,
author, journalist.

[3] Robert ('Bobbie' to Connolly, 'Bobby' to Kenneth Clark) Longden
(1903–40), Trinity classics 1922–6; Connolly's closest friend at Eton and
Oxford; killed in a wartime bombing raid on Wellington College, where he
was headmaster.

[4] Cf. 'That I at midnight by the clock / May creep into your bed' (W. B.
Yeats, 'The Three Bushes', *New Poems*, 1938).

The Late Lorn Lesbian

In memory of Thomas Hardy

Who are you that stand in a dinner-jacket,
  With monocled air
  And gentleman's hair,
With pants on instead of drawers or placket,
As if you were ready for some rare racket?

'I am one of those whom mankind calls queer,
  Though in Lesbos isle
  There was many a smile
For such as I am in yesteryear,
But today there are few to call me dear.'

Strange are the tricks of the purblind blender,
  Who planted thus
  Some dark Oedipus
In a breastless bosom, and will not mend a
Shuddering horror of male pudenda.

'Nay, in your sex are some like me.
  Choose your Nancy
  And pay your fancy
Till both the sexes are mixed may be,
And none can tell if it's he or she.'

1937

---

§ The poem's metrical form and vocabulary derive from those of its
dedicatee, Thomas Hardy (1840–1928). In the summer of 1937 Bowra was
briefly engaged to the masculine-looking lesbian Audrey Beecham (1915–89),
Somerville PPE 1934–7. The engagement prompted Bowra to remark 'Buggers
can't be choosers', but it was Audrey, allegedly after advice from Cyril
Connolly (19/2) and Robert Boothby (75/§), who backed out.

Uffington Downs

At Garrard's Farm, under the White Horse Hill,
Lived John and little Yellow[1] – daughter she
Of some famed general[2] in the Indian wars,
Who oft led redcoats to the battle-line,
And wore three rows of medals on his chest
For gallant service to our gracious Queen.
But John came from the sturdy middle class,[3]
Who from the strange intricacies of trade
Had laid a little nest-egg by, well placed
In consols and guilt-edged securities
With annual yield of three per cent. The twain
Lived happily on this, and gave their time
To social service and to daily deeds
Of kindness to the folk of White Horse Hill.
 Among his dog-eared books and coloured prints
Of hunting scenes and ancient monuments
And architectural piles in foreign climes
John would peruse the works of bygone men
And write great tomes of learning lightly borne;
Sunk in the past was he, but not afraid
To grapple with the present's many needs,
To play at cricket on the village green,

§ John Betjeman and his wife Penelope (1910–86) moved into Garrard's
Farm, Uffington, in the Vale of the White Horse, Berkshire, in 1934, the year
after their marriage. By 1935 Bowra had already started to taunt Betjeman
about the couple's childlessness. Their first child was not born until 1937, after
Penelope had stood on the eye of the White Horse and prayed to the pagan
gods for fertility: *New Fame, New Love* (xi/1), 91. Bowra's poetic
interpretation of these events is written in the style of Tennyson's *Idylls of the
King* (1859–85).

 [1] One of John Betjeman's many nicknames for Penelope.
 [2] Field Marshal Sir Philip Chetwode (1869–1950), Penelope Betjeman's
father, had been Commander-in-Chief of the British Army in India.
 [3] John Betjeman's father, Ernest, was the third generation of the family to
run Betjemann [*sic*] & Sons, furniture-makers.

To study miracles of gas and steam,
To take the village boys upon his knees
And tell improving stories, or to kiss
Their upturned innocent faces full of love.
But Yellow was more active in her ways.
She physicked horses when they had the thrush,
Or lectured to the Women's Institute,
Or knitted jerseys for the godly poor,
Or taught the middle classes how to cook,
Blancmange or rich red jellies or meringues,
Or put the clover[1] in the apple tart.
Each Lord's Day, when the Matins' summons rang,
The twain, in Sabbath godliness, would go
To Church, where Dr Harton[2] spoke of God.
Yellow would lead the trebles in the choir
To chants by Dykes or Stanford or by Monk,[3]
Whilst John, with deep resounding organ tones,
Would read from Numbers or Leviticus.
Nor failed they twice a year to take their share
Of bread and wine, spread neatly on a cloth
Upon an oaken table, whilst kind words
Came from good Dr Harton's reverent lips.

So passed they happily from day to day,
Nor found allurement from the thought of sin;
But that mysterious Providence, which guides
Our earthly journey, though it blessed them much,
Denied one blessing; for they had no child.

---

[1] The MS gives this instead of the expected but unrhythmical 'cloves'. If
not a slip of the pen, this may be a jocular reference to Penelope Betjeman's
capacity for putting the eating needs of her horse well before those of her
guests, who were often left to fend for themselves.

[2] The Revd Frederick Harton (1889–1958), at the time Vicar of Baulking, a
village near Uffington; close friend and spiritual adviser to the Betjemans.

[3] J(ohn) B. Dykes (1823–76), Sir Charles Stanford (1852–1924) and Edwin
Monk (1819–1900) were all notable composers of Anglican church
music.

They loved each other much, and every night
John would implant a kiss on Yellow's brow,
Or put his arms around her swelling bust,
Or play with her small hands – but still no child.
The village talked of it with sympathy,
But others, in whom riches had half-killed
The love of God, would talk with harsher tongues,
And say the fault lay or with her or John,
Right punishment for early years misspent.
And foremost midst these idle chatterers
Was she who reigned in a great country house,
Elizabethan-Gothic, full of plate
And aspidistras and mahogany,
The Lady Pakenham,[1] not herself well born
But married to a wealthy nobleman
And fully conscious of her new-found class.
Her talk would reach the happy pair, and oft
They spent the day in weeping over it,
That their sad want should be a cause for jests
And callous comments from the Upper Class.

One Easter Monday, at the great rich house
Where Viscount Pakenham swayed his wide estate,
A fête was held, with booths and roundabouts,
And Punch and Judy shows and tin toy trains.
To this went John and Yellow, well attired
In broadcloth he, in scarlet satin she,
To taste the simple pleasures of the poor.
Her Ladyship was there in all her pearls,
Clad in her new hand-woven mackintosh,

---

[1] Elizabeth (née Harman) (1906–2002), wife of Christ Church don Frank Pakenham (1905–2001), later Lord Longford; by 1937 already a mother of three. Despite Frank's aristocratic background, the description of the couple's grandiose surroundings given here is pure fantasy. Sending a copy of this poem to Jack Beddington in April 1938, Betjeman gave a truer picture of the Pakenhams' life-style: 'They are both Socialists and live in a horrible villa down the Iffley Road and eat Co-op food.' *Letters*, vol. 1 (xi/1), 208.

Surrounded by her company of beaux.
She listened to their airy badinage
And watched the stallions sporting with the mares;
For the rich lord was proud of his great stud
And bred up winners for the Derby Race.
To them came John and Yellow, ignorant
Of nature's simple means to propagate,
And saw the stallions sporting with the mares.
'Look! Look!' cried Yellow in her innocence,
'That horse is riding on the other's back!'
And turning to her Ladyship enquired:
'What are your horses doing over there?'
The Lady laughed and did not make reply,
While Yellow blushed and did not understand.
But John was pensive all the afternoon,
And missed three catches in the cricket-match,
Prey to some new and strange anxiety.

They came back to their cottage without talk,
And Yellow could not see what irked John so,
But did not like to ask him, for she feared
He might be meditating some high theme
Of Grace or Faith or words of Holy Writ.
Then suddenly John went out of the room,
And came back with some reins and snaffle-bit,
And bearing on his arm a mackintosh.
Mysteriously he addressed his wife:
'Come, let us see if God's will may be done.'
She, always faithful to her loving spouse,
Did just as she was bid, and loathed it not,
But found a new delight in solacing
John's strange new interest in natural things.

The months rolled by, and with them every day
Made Yellow's waistline show a broader curve,
And villagers with kindly nods would say
That Providence had blessed them after all.
So nine months passed, and then the happy twain

Added a third to their sweet company;
And at the church on Quinquagesima
Good Dr Harton held baptismal rites
And named the infant Paul Sylvester George,[1]
And Lady Pakenham gave a silver cup,
Embossed with scenes of Greek mythology,
And fifteen shillings in the Savings Bank.

1937

---

[1] Born 26 November 1937.

Lux Mundi

High on her Moty-car rides my Penelope,
   White as an Easter-egg under the stars.
      See the good clergyman riding beside her!
      Ah, he is longing to break her and ride her,
         Saddle her tightly, snaffle her lightly,
   Make her jump over the gate's five bars.

Loud in the Village Hall lectures Penelope –
   Slides of the Anglican Church in Nepal.
      All about Yogi her sweet tones are thrilling,
      How to make *blanquette de veau* for a shilling.
         Village girls crush on her, love the fresh flush
         on her.
Art and theology, she knows them all.

Low at the altar-rail kneels my Penelope,
   Pursed little lips turned up to her God,
      Thinking of Matins and Holy Communion,
      Breakfast at eight and the Fellowship Union.
         Freely God gave her It, made her his favourite;
He was the Father who put her in pod.

---

§ 'The light of the world'. This parody of John Betjeman's poem 'Myfanwy'
– in *Old Lights for New Chancels* (xxvi/3) – celebrates Penelope Betjeman,
whose main passions were religion, India and horses: her grey Arab gelding
Moti was treated like one of the family. A devoted Anglican until her
conversion to Roman Catholicism in 1948, Penelope transformed village life
(and galvanised Uffington's Women's Institute) by her energy and enthusiasm
for introducing cultural activities. During 1940 John Betjeman worked at the
Ministry of Information in London, leaving Penelope (and their son Paul)
alone in Uffington during the week.

Lone in her double-bed sleeps my Penelope,
  Dreaming of heaven and life with her Lord,
    How she will manage that company glorious,
    See that the descant is not too uproarious,
      Be life and soul of them, take full control of them,
  Next to our Father at bed and at board.

1940

RAF 1940

Will you please wind up the propeller?[1]
   We should like to go out for a spin.
There's an eighteenth-century rood-loft
   And some box-pews at King's Lynn,
And the Gothic Revival church at St Ivel
   Is better than all Berlin.

No, we never fly on a Sunday;
   Our padre thinks it not right.
The boys are most keen on the service,
   And the Corporal's an acolyte.
He's a dear little chap in his blue forage-cap,
   And his name is Merrivale White.[2]

There aren't any girls in the barracks;
   We feel that they might spoil the fun.
We much prefer sketching and fretwork
   To fooling about with a gun,
And as for this flying and killing and dying,
   We leave all that stuff to the Hun.

1940

---

§ Since John Betjeman's attempts to join the RAF in 1939–40 were
unsuccessful, this poem (in typical Betjeman rhythm) is pure fantasy, reflecting
his architectural enthusiasms, religious commitment and earlier pacifist
inclinations.

  [1] 'Propeller' was another of Betjeman's nicknames for his wife.

  [2] The homoerotic poems of the Revd E. E. Bradford, which Betjeman
much enjoyed, include an account of the unexpected propositioning of an
older man by 'A shy little fellow called Merrivale White': 'At Last!', in *The
New Chivalry and Other Poems*, 1918. Betjeman wrote some homoerotic poems
himself: one such presumably juvenile work, now in the Archive of Magdalen
College, Oxford (and unpublished as this volume goes to press), dwells on the
messily physical aspects of a sexual encounter between two schoolboys rather
than the aesthetic admiration of the older man for the younger that normally
characterises Bradford's verses.

Dr Zaehner

On the great eight-cornered table
  Lies an ever-open tome
Where the tongues of men and angels
  Keep an everlasting home.
Foolish prefix, foolish suffix,
  Foolish verbs in Sog and Zend,[1]
You may think that you can cheat him –
  Prof. will get you in the end.
    Brother Thomas, Brother Thomas,[2]
      Oh! the hoary sack of sin,
    Comes to visit Dr Zaehner
      For a morning tot of gin.

On his stately Swiss piano
  Prof. can play with either hand.
Hearken to the swelling pedals –
  Berlioz on the demi-grand!
Let his Lordship[3] bag the pedal,
  He will pay for it in full;
Prof. is lord of all the music
  In his palace beautiful.

---

§ The subject is Robert Zaehner (1913–74), of Swiss descent; Senior Scholar, Christ Church, 1937–9; thereafter Research Lecturer. An oriental linguist specialising in Persian, Armenian and Zend, he developed a deep interest in Zoroastrianism and other Eastern religions and went on to become Spalding Professor of Eastern Religions and Ethics at Oxford in 1952. Usually known as 'Prof.', he was an excellent pianist.

[1] Sogdian is a dead Iranian language and Zend an ancient Persian religious tongue spoken by Zoroastrians.

[2] 'Brother Thomas More' was the name in religion of H. F. ('Adrian') Bishop (c.1898–1942; see also p. xxviii and 50/§).

[3] Gerald Tyrwhitt-Wilson (1883–1950), 14th Baron Berners, composer, author and eccentric, who lived at Faringdon House in Berkshire.

Lady Prudence, Lady Prudence,[1]
Oh! her suit of corduroy,
Dances round with Dr Zaehner,
He the girl and she the boy.

Clever dons and Dean of Christ Church,
Watch that minus-thirteen eye![2]
'Neath the telescopic lenses
Lurks the spider for the fly.
Ahriman[3] is there to help him,
All the planets on his side.
You may think he does not notice;
Change your minds – or woe betide!
Mickey Rooney, Mickey Rooney,[4]
Oh the pleasant sight to see,
In the dark at the Electra[5]
Sits on Dr Zaehner's knee.[6]

1940

---

[1] Lady Prudence Pelham (1910–52), daughter of the 6th Earl of Chichester; sculptor and student of lettering with Eric Gill; a notable beauty who suffered early widowhood during the Second World War and died young of multiple sclerosis.

[2] Zaehner's very poor eyesight was corrected by thick spectacles; 'minus-thirteen' presumably refers to his prescription.

[3] The spirit of evil in Zoroastrian mythology, believed to live between the earth and the fixed stars.

[4] Mickey Rooney (b. 1920), Hollywood film star as a child and, less successfully, as a diminutive adult (who married eight times).

[5] A cinema in Queen Street, Oxford, demolished in 1958.

[6] An echo of Charles Kingsley: 'Airly Beacon, Airly Beacon, [. . .] With his baby on my knee!' 'Airly Beacon', *Andromeda and Other Poems*, 1858.

Major Prophet

Piled on the gorgeous russet carpet
   Are Russian texts of Marx and Verne;[1]
From Tel Aviv the radio's calling,
   The gas fire and the electric burn.
In asymmetrical relations
   He can distinguish S from P;
He is the class of all the classes,
   The final flower of PPE.
      From Riga, Prague and Nuffield College
      Gathers the Philosophenbund
      With Rachmilevich,[2] Count Zamoyski,[3]
      Katkov,[4] Hourani,[5] Wiesengrund.[6]

§ This poem is a parody of Betjeman's 'Dorset' (in *Continual Dew*, 1937),
which is itself modelled on Thomas Hardy's 'Friends Beyond' (in *Wessex
Poems and Other Verses*, 1898). Its subject is Bowra's friend Isaiah Berlin
(1909–97), at that time a philosopher and Fellow of New College; Berlin was a
committed Zionist and a knowledgeable music-lover.

[1] Berlin's first book, published in 1939, had been on Karl Marx; a Russian
translation of the works of Jules Verne had been among his favourite
childhood reading.

[2] Solomon Rachmilevich (*c.*1892–1952), Berlin's first intellectual mentor;
both were Russian-Jewish and originally from Riga.

[3] Count Andrzej Zamoyski (1905–64), Polish by birth but brought up in
England, and at the time of this poem living near Oxford; keenly interested in
philosophy, which he had studied in Crakow.

[4] George Katkov (1903–85), Russian philosopher; an academic in Prague
before emigrating to England in 1939.

[5] Albert Hourani (1915–93), Magdalen PPE 1933–6, later became an
authority on the history of the Middle East.

[6] Theodor Ludwig Wiesengrund Adorno (1903–69), German philosopher
and musicologist, left Germany in 1934 and studied in Oxford until 1938, when
he moved to the US.

Hark to the early English music,
    Byrd's motet for a single string!
See the young girls' enraptured faces
    To the adagio listening.
Oh, hark, for sex-appeal is calling
    And ripples down those bended necks.
The master calls them to attention,
    Unveils the mysteries of sex.
        What would they give to call him husband,
            To pluck the roses from his lips,
        With Mrs Halpern,[1] Mary Fisher,[2]
            The Granta,[3] both the Lynds[4] and Tips?[5]

But in the bluest blood of Riga
    Pulsates a redder, stronger wine.
In Palm Beach suiting, sola topi,
    Isaiah rides to Palestine.
Solomon's temple rises for him,
    The minions of the Mufti fall.
The new Messiah stands conducting
    Beethoven by the Wailing Wall.

---

[1] Barbara Halpern, née Strachey (1912–99), LMH history 1930–3, followed a career at the BBC.

[2] Mary Fisher (b. 1913), later Bennett, Somerville classics 1931–5, Principal, St Hilda's, 1965–80.

[3] Shiela Grant Duff (1913–2004), LMH PPE 1931–4, foreign correspondent and writer on Czechoslovakia. The Granta is a tributary of the Cam, which runs through Cambridge.

[4] The sisters Sigle ('Sheila') and Maire ('Moira') Lynd, famed for their beauty. Sigle (1910–76) briefly read chemistry and biology at Somerville 1929–30; Maire (1912–90) was a Home Student reading classics 1930–4. Both joined the Communist Party.

[5] Rachel Walker (1913–92), Somerville PPE 1931–4, a pupil of Berlin's who fell in love with him. She later became mentally ill.

Though Coupland[1] show a pair of aces,
    Full House with jacks and jokers wins,
With Stephen Spender,[2] Uncle Isaac,[3]
    One Frankfurter[4] and both Berlins.[5]

1940

---

[1] Reginald Coupland (1884–1952), Beit Professor of the History of the British Empire, Oxford, 1920–48; member of the Peel Commission on Palestine 1936–7.

[2] The poet and critic (1909–95), Berlin's close friend, was partly Jewish by descent.

[3] Yitzhak Samunov (1886–1950), husband of Berlin's maternal aunt Ida; a fervent Zionist who settled in Palestine.

[4] Felix Frankfurter (1882–1965), American-Jewish lawyer, George Eastman Visiting Professor at Oxford 1933–4, Associate Justice of the US Supreme Court 1939–62.

[5] Presumably Berlin's parents, Mendel and Marie, both of whom (Marie with particular enthusiasm) were Zionists.

Air Populaire

Loud on every Oxford steeple
    Rings the merry Christmas chime:
'Happy husbands, love the people,
    All the people all the time!'
See the townsmen shout and stare,
Thunderstruck by Mrs Ayer.[1]

Not a manger in a stable
    But a nursery for two,
With a pouf, a gate-legged table,
    And two chairs of Reckitt's blue.
Julian and Valerie,[2] say,
Who shall be your dad to-day.

Softly from his sleeping Billa
    Slips the fascinated Roy,[3]
Creeping off to Renée's villa;
    She'll provide him with a boy.[4]
There is lots and lots of room
In that hospitable womb.

---

§ Apparently intended to be sung to Henry Gauntlett's 1849 melody for 'Once in Royal David's City'.

[1] Renée Ayer (1909–80), née Lees, had married philosopher A. J. ('Freddie') Ayer in 1932; they were divorced in 1942, and Renée married Stuart Hampshire in 1961. Isaiah Berlin described Bowra as 'impulsively generous' to her in 1939–40: loc. cit. (xix/1), fo. 129.

[2] Valerie Ayer (1936–81), daughter of Renée and Freddie Ayer, and Julian Ayer (1939–2004), son of Renée Ayer and Stuart Hampshire, but brought up as the son of Freddie Ayer.

[3] Economist Roy Harrod (1900–78), Student of Christ Church 1924–67, and his wife Wilhelmine ('Billa') (1911–2005), née Cresswell.

[4] Fantasy.

One goes out, in comes another;
   Husbands play at Box and Cox.
Perfect wife and perfect mother,
   Making love and making socks –
Still they whisper in Japan:
'She's the girl for every man.'

She will have her boys in khaki,
   She will have her boys in blue.
Poor Eliza,[1] poor Miss Starkie,[2]
   What a chance on earth have you?
All the wandering hearts of men
Come to roost at last with Ren.

She may shrink from Dr Zaehner,[3]
   She may shrink from I. Berlin;[4]
Dons may foolishly disdain her,
   But the great big world comes in.
Weary warriors flock to rest
On that universal breast.

If the rate of births is falling,
   She'll make up with quads and quins.
Boys, you hear your duty calling;
   Now the heroic task begins.
Form up with the People's Front,
Form up for a bit of c—

1940

---

[1] According to John Sparrow, this refers to Elizabeth Pakenham, a famous
beauty (23/1 and pp. xxiv, xxix).
[2] Enid Starkie (1897–1970), Lecturer in French Literature and Fellow,
Somerville College.
[3] 29/§.
[4] Isaiah Berlin (31/§).

Ballad

What is the bird that sings in your breast?
  Lord Berners,[1] oh, tell me, oh!
Is it a cuckoo that fouls a nest
Or a cock of the walk with scarlet crest
  That is fair and fine to see, oh?

'Three times every night my cock has crowed,
  Crowed on the topmost C, oh!
And its song has been heard in the Woodstock Road,
As loud as the voice of Lady Wode,[2]
  But never a note of glee, oh!'

At daybreak I saw a red cock rise
  To a height that none could see, oh!
It flapped its wings in the morning skies
And fluttered my heart with a wild surmise.
  Can such your songster be, oh?

'No bird of mine was ever so red,
  Alack and the woe to me, oh!
The bird that nests in my heart is dead.
Its weight is the weight of a load of lead,
  And it brings me dule and dree, oh!'

---

§ Bowra sent a copy of this poem to John Sparrow on 18 July 1940,
commenting 'You will remember that Lord B. was told by his analist [*sic*] that
he had a dead bird in him. That, and the dialogue form, should explain all
that is necessary for an educated man!'

[1] 29/3.
[2] Hester ('Star') Chetwode (1871–1946), mother of Penelope Betjeman.

Does it come like a dream from the Ivory Gate[1]
    When the moon is low on the lea, oh?
Or does it warble a hymn of hate
Such as children sing when their parents mate
    And love flows like foam of the sea, oh!?

'My bird is locked in a dateless gloom
    And will never again be free, oh!
Its voice is a voice that comes from the tomb;
Its burden is, "Back, come back to the womb!",
    And thither soon shall I flee, oh!'

1940

---

[1] In Greek mythology, dreams came from the realm of Morpheus (the god of dreams) – false ones through the Ivory Gate, true ones through the Gate of Horn.

On the Reform of a Ministry

With queens, ambassadors, and Kenneth Clark,
Reith sank dishonoured to the outer dark,
And Duff interprets all that England means
With Kenneth Clark, ambassadors and queens.

9 August 1940

---

§ Inspired by Hilaire Belloc's epigram 'On a General Election', this poem commemorates the personnel changes in the Ministry of Information during 1940. Sir John Reith (1889–1971), previously the first Director-General of the BBC, was appointed Minister on 5 January, but was replaced by the politician and diplomat Duff Cooper (1890–1954) on 12 May. Kenneth Clark remained there from 1939 to 1941.

The Silent Column

Not a murmur, not a sound!
   Let no syllable be said!
Quislings listen underground;
   Spies are hid in every bed.
In procession slow and solemn
Marches on the silent column.

Once perhaps heard sounds were sweet,
   Now unheard are sweeter far.[1]
Silent invocations greet
   Barmen at the MI[2] bar.
When was tune more dulcet carolled
Than the song unsung by Harold?

Now his rosy lips are sealed,
   Greet the strong and silent one;
Now our leader is revealed,
   Hail to holy Nicolson.
See the Saviour is uprisen
Follow him, or go to prison.

---

§ Harold Nicolson (14/5) was Duff Cooper's Parliamentary Secretary at
the Ministry of Information 1940–1. On 15 July 1940, in an effort to reduce
rumour and gossip at a time when fear of a Fifth Column in Britain was at
its height, the Ministry published prominent newspaper advertisements
exhorting people to 'Join Britain's Silent Column' and not to pass on
information about bombing-raids.

[1] Cf. 'Heard melodies are sweet, but those unheard / Are sweeter.' Keats,
'Ode on a Grecian Urn', 1819–20.

[2] Ministry of Information.

Now no more the soaring Clark[1]
  Sings to greet the movie star;
Betjeman preaching in the Park[2]
  Clamours silently for war.
Harold, high in heav'n or near it,
Blazons a new holy spirit.

Once he had the gift of tongues –
  Old Mortality[3] can tell.
Strange potations filled his lungs
  Sipped from loneliness's well.[4]
But now anything is sweeter
Than to ope his mouth to Vita.[5]

[1] Perhaps an echo of Shelley's lark, which 'singing still dost soar, and soaring ever singest' ('To a Skylark', 1820). Kenneth Clark had recently moved from being Director of the Ministry of Information's Films Division to a post controlling Home Publicity.

[2] On Sunday 21 July 1940 Harold Nicolson spoke at a 'Rout the Rumour Rally' held in Hendon Park. John Betjeman, a member of the Ministry's Films Division, presumably spoke too, since in the copy Bowra sent to Sylvester Gates (apparently an earlier draft; see p. xiii) these lines read 'London calling through the dark / Dumbly stimulates to war'; 'This is London calling' was how the BBC World Service introduced its broadcasts.

[3] Raymond Mortimer (1895–1980), critic, author and editor, was on the staff of the Ministry of Information 1940–1.

[4] *The Well of Loneliness,* a lesbian novel by Radclyffe Hall, had been published in 1928 and banned on grounds of obscenity.

[5] Cf. 'Any thing to me is sweeter / Than to see shock-headed Peter.' Anonymous English translation (in *The English Struwwelpeter, or Pretty Stories and Funny Pictures for Little Children,* 1848) of the title poem in Heinrich Hoffmann's *Der Struwwelpeter, oder lustige Geschichten und drollige Bilder für Kinder von 3 bis 6 Jahren* ('Shock-headed Peter, or merry stories and funny pictures for children from 3 to 6 years'), 1847 (first published under a version of its alternative title, 1845). Victoria (Vita) Sackville-West (1892–1962), wife of Harold Nicolson, was, like him, bisexual.

Other columns once were his,[1]
Rising, rising in the night,
But no column brought such bliss,
Shone with such angelic light.
Like St Simeon,[2] he can fill a
World with visions round a pillar.

Praise him as erect he stands,
Balliol boys of nineteen-eight,[3]
Lift to him your hearts and hands,
Praise him in his solemn state.
Sharpen tools to help the master
Make his column rise up faster.

27 July 1940

---

[1] Nicolson had been closely allied to Oswald Mosley and was a member of his New Party before Mosley turned to Fascism.
[2] St Simeon Stylites (390–459), who passed his life in self-mortification on top of increasingly high pillars.
[3] Nicolson had been an undergraduate at Balliol 1904–7.

Sir John's Wedding

A Berkshire legend

Sir John de Betjeman rides apace
And gladness gleams on his high-born face;
His milk-white teeth and his wine-dark hair
Are an answer to every maiden's prayer.

On his red roan steed he has coursed for miles,
And little he recks of his new-born piles,
And little he recks of the long white road;
For he dreams of his lady, Penelope Wode.

He found her under a chestnut-tree,
And reading a Book of Hours was she.
His heart went pit and his heart went pat
For desire of the maid he was gazing at.

And now he rides over valley and down
To the Church of St Peter in Uffington town,
And Father Folky awaits him there
To give the Host to the bridal pair.

The Chetwodes stand in the crowded aisle
And broad is Lady de Chetwode's smile.

---

§ The originals of the characters in this romantic fantasy, written in the
style of Richard Barham's *Ingoldsby Legends* (1840–7), are the distinctly non-
equestrian John Betjeman (15/§), his father Ernest Betjemann (1872–1934)
and mother Bess Betjeman [*sic*] (1878–1952); Penelope Chetwode (21/§, 26/§),
her father Sir Philip Chetwode (21/2) and mother Hester (36/2); the
Revd Frederick Harton (22/2) ('Father Folky') and his wife Sybil (1898–1993)
('Abbess Sybil'). In reality John Betjeman had married Penelope Chetwode in
some secrecy in 1933; although his parents attended, hers were not told until
some weeks later.

For she knows that never was lordlier son
Than Sir Ernie's first-born, the gay Sir John.

Sir Ernie lies 'neath a distant sod,
And Masses are said for his soul to God;
But the wife of his bosom, the good Dame Bess,
Guides the son of his loins in all godliness.

The Abbess Sybil has tuned the keys
And unfolded the hymnal over her knees;
For anthems must hallow the silken bed
Of the lovely couple who come to be wed.

Sir John has cantered the west door through
And stabled his horse in an oak box-pew;
He has thrown his cap to a singing-boy,
And the Chetwodes lift up their hearts for joy.

The Abbess Sibyl, with russet hair,
On the clavichord strikes an old-time air;
Her song is loud in that holy place,
But louder is Baron de Chetwode's bass.

But oh, why does Father Folky pale,
And why do the Abbess's fingers fail?
And why does Lady de Chetwode lurch
Like a ship in the sea through the crowded church?

Why does good Dame Bess in her crimson gown
Tear her hair that is white as the white swandown,
And murmur: 'A wedding awaits my John,
But where has the Lady Penelope gone?'

The hinds and the maids from the village green
Look round in vain for their May Day queen,

For the rose-red lips and the red-gold hair –
The Lady Penelope is not there.

'Perchance she has taken her mare for a ride,
Or milks the goats at a farmer's side.
But has she forgotten a day like this
And the lordling who waits to take her in bliss?'

But hark, for a rustle of limbs is heard
And lips fall dumb on a half-said word;
For a maiden stands in the Lord's Day light;
Her voice is loud and her eyes are bright.

Golden the curls round her head that fly,
Golden the eyelash over her eye;
And what would a man not give to share
The golden night of her pubic hair?

Each little tit like a half grapefruit
Swells rosily forth from its firm-set root;
Each little buttock rises and falls
With the crisp curved movement of tennis balls.

But sweeter than buttock or bursting breast
Is her voice, of all voices the loveliest;[1]
Like a Siren calling, it rises high
And bewitches all who are standing by.

'I never shall marry the knight Sir John;
God says I am never to let him on.
My chaste limbs shrink from a bed abhorred;
I shall wed with none but the living Lord.'

---

[1] Penelope Betjeman's voice was distinctive, and was described variously as
'a shrill whine', 'a tremendous drawl' and a 'penetrating upper-class cockney'
with a timbre 'like that of a Punch-and-Judy man using his swazzle'. *Young
Betjeman* (xxv/2), 370, 373, 368.

'What lord can she speak of?' cried Bess forlorn,
'For I wot that my John is nobly born.'
'What she needs is the birch,' cried Lady Wode,
'To teach her to walk in the narrow road.'

The Chetwodes quaked in a mad alarm,
And the Baron bared his wild, white arm,
And Sir John in a frenzy of black despair
Clasped the hand of a choirboy kneeling there.

The maids and the hinds of the White Horse Hill
Turned pale with a presage of untold ill,
And Bess sank down on the red-tiled floor
As a tired cow sinks at the cowhouse door.

And Lady Wode, like a mad March day,
Cried: 'This is a sin for which she shall pay.
In the family gaol I shall lock her up,
And water and bread shall be all her sup.'

But the Lady Penelope stood unstirred,
And her red lips uttered never a word.
Her eyes were upturned to the roof above
And their light was the light of unearthly love.

Then lo, she was lifted before their eyes
And rose like a lark in the April skies;
And all around her there danced a light
Such as breaks through a chancel-window bright.

Up she flew through the beams of the Gothic fane,
And never on earth was she seen again,
But high in the belfry a voice rang free:
'I go to a Lord who is worthy me.'

Sir John de Betjeman fell on his knees
And thanked the Lord for His high decrees,
And all the Chetwodes and good Dame Bess
Knelt and praised the Lord in his Holiness.

This tale did I hear on the White Horse Down
From a greybeard yokel of Uffington town.
And, all ye good Christians, remember to pray
For my soul on St Penelope's Day.

8 August 1940

Captain Courageous

'Wot's orl the foocking fooss abaht?'
  Asked Boynton from his bed.
'To get yer out, to get yer out,'
  The Sergeant-Major said.
'The Captain's in for trouble;
So get up at the double,
  And show yer bloody 'ead.'

'He likes to poke his person where
  I'd 'ate to put my stick.
And I won't 'ave no bottoms bare
  For such as 'im to prick.
The Army Acts forbid it,
And 'im what's gone and did it,
  Must pay up bloody quick.'

The Captain's stuck upon the mat,
  And guilt is in his eye.
He knows that all who sin like that
  Disgrace the Old School Tie,
That he who tries to fuck a
Lance-Corporal isn't pukka
  And suffers by and by.

---

§ This imaginative work, whose title recalls Rudyard Kipling's 1897
adventure story *Captains Courageous* and is a parody of the same author's
'Danny Deever' (in *Barrack-Room Ballads and Other Verses*, 1892), was inspired
by John Sparrow (14/2), an enthusiastic homosexual. Sparrow joined up at
the start of the Second World War and was transferred to the Holding
Battalion of the Coldstream Guards, based at Regent's Park Barracks, in May
1940. Kit Boynton was his batman there.

The Company Commander takes
   His sjambok from the wall,
And sweet, oh sweet the sound it makes
   To all who know the Call.
The lithe lash sweeps on singing,
And mercilessly ringing
   Blows on bare buttocks fall.

The Subalterns cry 'Tally-ho!'
   And join the general fun.
They laugh to see him wobble so
   And watch the fresh blood run.
With hunting-horns resounding
And blow on blow rebounding
   They show him how it's done.

'I know a trick worth two of that,'
   The brave Old Colonel cries:
'Let's chuck him in the midden, what,
   And give him a surprise.
Now, all together, heave him
Into the shit, and leave him
   To find out where he lies.'

The Captain crawls out of the pool.
   His bleeding arse is bare.
There's shit upon his guilty tool,
   And shit upon his hair.
His eyes are red with weeping,
And feebly he comes creeping,
   While all the neighbours stare.

Before the stately mansion's door
   His white-haired father stands;
His mother writhes upon the floor,
   His sisters wring their hands.

Of those who wait to meet him
Will none come forth to greet him?
  Is none who understands?

His good old father prays to God
  To ease his hopeless grief;
But when a man's son is a sod,
  What prayer can bring relief?
With steps that fail and falter
His will he goes to alter;
  His time, he knows, is brief.

The Captain takes his jack-knife out;
  He has a task to do.
His heart is high, his courage stout,
  His blade is clean and true.
Then murmuring softly 'Finis',
He slices off his penis
  And both his bollocks too.

He takes the trophy to the Mess
  In slow and solemn state.
The Colonel in all courtliness
  Welcomes the pious freight.
With name inscribed of donor
It gets the place of honour
  In the regimental plate.

In Regent's Park when wars are few
  And winter nights are long,
The Colonel and his jovial crew
  Their youthfulness prolong.
And in the loud beâno
The Captain's shrill soprano
  Merrily leads the song.

17 March 1941

[49]

Old Croaker

O stark, stark, stark amid the blaze of June,
Uncoveredly stark,[1]
With broad black hips artificially sunburnt
And rubicund lips that challenge the tomato.
Brown shorts, brown necks that encumber the Metro,
Sidelong glances down Unter den Linden.

---

§ To call this poem a parody is inadequate: it is Bowra's response to the
poetry of T. S. Eliot and a recognition of its impact on poetry in general. The
title refers to 'East Coker' (1940), the second of Eliot's *Four Quartets*, but the
substance of the poem is modelled on *The Waste Land* (1922) and *Ash
Wednesday* (1930) and their vast range of allusion to European literature in
general: echoes emerge here of Milton, W. B. Yeats, Coleridge, Rimbaud,
Byron, Thomas Nashe, Swinburne, Tennyson, James Joyce, several of
Shakespeare's plays and one of his sonnets, popular songs from different eras,
lyrics from the stage, cinema and music hall, and nursery rhymes. Alongside
these secular references runs a parallel thread of religious quotation – parodied
phrases from the Bible, from prayers and from the liturgy, and from a hymn
by Cardinal Newman. Some of the passages alluded to are quoted at the
beginning of the notes that follow, but the links to *The Waste Land* are in
general left for the reader to explore.

The subject of the poem is Bowra's friend Adrian Bishop (29/2 and p. xxviii).
Vigorously homosexual, Bishop introduced Bowra to the homosexual
subculture of Berlin during Bowra's two-term sabbatical from Wadham in
1932. After a brief spell living near the Betjemans' home in Uffington, Bishop
suffered a serious illness in 1936, underwent a religious conversion, and
entered an Anglican monastery. When war broke out he was released from his
vows to enter the intelligence services, and died mysteriously at a hotel in
Tehran in 1942.

Although London, Paris and Athens, where Bowra and Bishop also spent
time, are fleetingly visited in the poem, its main roots lie in Berlin: that city's
familiar landmarks – Unter den Linden, the Wannsee lake, the Underground,
and the suburb of Spandau (notorious for its prison) – overlie the specialised
attractions of the boy-bars which would have been familiar to Bishop and
Bowra, as they were to the poet W(ystan) H. Auden (1907–73) and the writer
Christopher Isherwood (1904–86), both mentioned in the poem. Against this is
set the monastic life to which Bishop temporarily retreated.

[1] 'O dark, dark, dark, amid the blaze of noon, / Irrecoverably dark.'
Milton, *Samson Agonistes*, 1671.

Baronin Fould-Springer[1] of a first-rate family
Said to be the fattest woman in Europe
Went to bed with a dud Czech
Who talked French with a real French accent.
He froze all her assets,
And the psychologist takes over her guilt-edged securities.

I will arise and go now and go to have a pee,
Way down in Innisfree.[2]
That's where I wish to be
With a Corporal on my knee.
Oh is it town or gown or tousled hair,
A tousled boy-scout's hair
Inside the WC?

Over the Wannsee
    The saxophone
Plays, How do you do, do,
    Mister Brown?[3]

An evzone with harmonica
In a ginshop once I saw,[4]
Leonidas,[5] a Spartan lad,

---

[1] The immensely rich but not excessively fat Austrian Baroness Marie-Cécile
('Mary' or 'Mitzi') Springer (1886–1978), who married first Baron Eugène
Fould (whereupon they merged their surnames), then after his death Frank
Wooster, allegedly her late husband's lover; mother-in-law of Bowra's friend
Alan Pryce-Jones (57/3).
[2] 'I will arise and go now, and go to Innisfree.' W. B. Yeats, 'The Lake Isle
of Innisfree', in *The Rose*, 1893.
[3] 'How do you do, Mr Brown?', a foxtrot from the 1932 musical comedy
film *Yes, Mr Brown*.
[4] 'A damsel with a dulcimer / In a vision once I saw.' Samuel Taylor
Coleridge, *Kubla Khan*, 1816. Evzones are soldiers in the Greek Army
belonging to a special corps known for its skirted ceremonial dress (and
allegedly willing, for a price, to satisfy visitors' curiosity about what is
underneath their skirts).
[5] The name of the king of Sparta who died as a hero at the Battle of
Thermopylae in 480 BC while defending Greece against Persian invaders.

And was he eager to be had,
Or was he?

He laid his dentures carefully on the shelf,
Lifted his skirts up just to give a peep,
And in sublime oblivion of self
Began to snore in regimental sleep.
The marble goddess on the Acropolis
Appreciates his natural good taste;
And when he leaves his bed to have a piss,
Protects his penis from unnatural waste.
Goldstein[1] is in Bohème or Silhouette,[2]
His cigarette-case of synthetic jade.
He cautiously selects the best tapette[3]
Who still is overworked if underpaid.
His Schaumwein[4] bubbles in a Lalique[5] glass
From which an aphrodisiac peeps out.
He makes a nicely calculated pass,
And Putzi understands what he's about.
The bar-attendant orders drinks all round,
The tango summons to the dancing-floor.
The last train passes on the Underground –
He slips behind the lavatory door.
Shanks's Patent, Barrhead,[6] watches his caresses;
Response is poor and standard rates are high;
Without ado he rapidly undresses
And promises to pay up by and by.

---

[1] Perhaps a generic reference to a punter, as Putzi may be to the boy prostitute he hires.

[2] Berlin night-clubs.

[3] Homosexual, in this case a prostitute.

[4] Sparkling wine.

[5] French designer René Lalique (1860–1945), famous for his distinctive glassware.

[6] The firm of Shanks & Co. of Barrhead were pioneers in sanitary ware.

Little Jack Horner
Sat in Cosy Corner
Pretending to be pi,[1]
Asked me to take him for a honeymoon at Venice,
To the Vier Jahreszeiten[2] with Wystan Auden.
Kennen Sie Christopher Isherwood?[3]
Of course I just live for art and music.
Oh for a night in Bohemia, lady.[4]
Yessir, I'm your Dadie,
I'm your Dadie now.[5]

Lead, blindly tight, amid the revolving room;
I'm tight and stark, fed up and far from home.[6]
Das ist die Liebe der Matrosen.[7]
Ô maisons, Ô gateaux,
Je cherche un matelot.[8]
You called me baby-doll a year ago.[9]
But Dr Zaehner[10] in the heather-bloom
Blindly explores the owner's sitting-room;

---

[1] 'Little Jack Horner / Sat in the corner, / Eating a Christmas pie' (nursery rhyme). Cosy Corner was a working-class bar on Zossenerstraße, where boy prostitutes plied for trade; a favourite haunt of Christopher Isherwood and his friends (now a dentist's surgery). 'Pi' means pious.

[2] A Berlin hotel near Unter den Linden.

[3] 'Do you know Christopher Isherwood?'

[4] The 1916 musical play *The Happy Day* includes the song 'Oh for a night in Bohemia'.

[5] 'Yes, sir, that's my baby, / No, sir, don't mean maybe, / Yes, sir, that's my baby now' (popular song, 1925). 'Dadie' is Bowra's friend George ('Dadie') Rylands (1902–99), Fellow of King's College, Cambridge 1927–99, University Lecturer in English, Cambridge, 1935–62; actor and theatre director.

[6] 'Lead, kindly Light, amid the encircling gloom, [. . .] The night is dark, and I am far from home.' Hymn by John Henry Newman, 1833.

[7] A German song ('That's how sailors love').

[8] 'O houses, O cakes, I'm looking for a sailor.' Cf. 'Ô saisons, ô châteaux, / Quelle âme est sans défauts?' ('O seasons, O castles, what soul is faultless?'). Arthur Rimbaud, 'Ô saisons, ô châteaux', in *Vers nouveaux et chansons*, 1872.

[9] From 'A Broken Doll', a popular song of 1916.

[10] 29/§.

Minus Thirteen[1] eludes the closet door
And leaves his Abendessen[2] on the floor.

At Hyde Park Corner
   The buses stop.
His Majesty's forces
   Like a drop.

Miles in the singular
   Common and supine,
But the plural cases
   Are always masculine.[3]

I want to go back, I want to go back,
I want to go back to my bed[4]
With Faivre cachets[5] in my head.

At Spandau then I came.[6]

Prevent us, O Lord, prevent us
In all our wooings.[7]

---

[1] 30/2.

[2] 'Evening meal'.

[3] 'Diës in the Singular / Common [sc. masc. or fem.] we define: / But its Plural cases are / always Masculine.' Gender rhyme in Benjamin Hall Kennedy, *The Revised Latin Primer*, 1888, 225.

[4] 'You gotta get up, you gotta get up, you gotta get up in the morning.' From Irving Berlin's First World War song, 'Oh! How I hate to get up in the morning', 1918.

[5] Dr Faivre's cachets – a form of medicine capsule – were alleged to offer protection against colds and headache. 'Faivre' appears in the version quoted by Noel Annan (see xi/1); the manuscript has 'fèvre' ('fever').

[6] 'To Carthage then I came.' T. S. Eliot, *The Waste Land*, quoting St Augustine's *Confessions*.

[7] 'Prevent us, O Lord, in all our doings.' Collect, communion service, *Book of Common Prayer*, 1662.

II

Because there is no cash but only credit;
Because there is no credit but only credit
Because there is no cash,
Because it is more blessed to give than to take,[1]
I will not give but forgive,
Take and not forsake,
Take what is yours and ours for our, your sake.
Lord, grant us to forgive
Those who do not take but give.
Forgive us our creditors as we forgive
Their credit against us.[2]

Prey on us now and in the hour of our debt.[3]

At the first vision of his golden hair
Would you not suddenly turn and stare?
Stand at the corner, light a cigarette,
Pretend your thoughts are neither here nor there,
Remark that the weather is neither fine nor wet,
Slip upon orange-peel or banana-skin,
Ready to take part in a tennis-set,
Go roller-skating in the Winter Garden,
Take lessons on the piano or mandoline,
Help his old mother take the washing in.

There is no alcohol in the soda-fountain
But only soda.
Give a Pernod to the poor old Guy.[4]

---

[1] 'It is more blessed to give than to receive.' Acts 20: 35.
[2] 'Forgive us our trespasses as we forgive those who trespass against us.' Matthew 18: 23.
[3] 'Pray for us now and at the hour of our death.' T. S. Eliot, *Ash Wednesday*, quoting from the Rosary and other prayers.
[4] The subtitle of T. S. Eliot's *The Hollow Men* (1925) is 'A Penny for the Old Guy'.

Where is the Fernet Branca[1] I bought
To share in Paris with a mobled queen?[2]
The Korn[3] King's court is empty, the Dantziger
    Goldwasser[4]
Stands on the counter unopened.
At the Tour d'Argent[5] the duck is not what it was.
Put on the lights and then put on the lights.[6]
That's the worst of these cheap cars.
What have I done to deserve all this?
What have I done?

White sails blowing on a windy sea.[7]
There's chicory in the coffee, the outboard motor leaks.
The Captain, sir, is in delirium.[8]
The isles of Greece, the isles of Greece[9]
Where Mr Eumorfopoulos[10] an Andriote merchant
Keeps a country house in the English fashion
With sun-dried octopus and rose-leaf jam.
Et dans le brouhaha
On dansait le polka.[11]

Poor Tom's a-cold.[12]

---

[1] A bitter, aromatic Italian liqueur sometimes used optimistically as a hangover cure.

[2] 'But who, O! who had seen the mobled queen –': Shakespeare, *Hamlet* II ii.

[3] A type of schnapps, often drunk as a beer-chaser.

[4] A German liqueur flavoured with caraway seeds, orange peel and spices, and containing minute flecks of gold leaf.

[5] A restaurant in Paris specialising in duck.

[6] 'Put out the light, and then put out the light.' Shakespeare, *Othello* V ii.

[7] Perhaps a memory of the yacht encountered by Bishop and Bowra in Corfu, and on which they travelled, Bishop for a year and Bowra in the summers of 1932 and 1933, on the second occasion buffeted by the north-east wind (*Memories*, 283, 285).

[8] 'My brother he is in Elysium.' Shakespeare, *Twelfth Night* I ii.

[9] Byron, 'The Isles of Greece', *Don Juan*, 1821, Canto 3, 86.

[10] George Eumorfopoulos (1863–1939) was a British collector of Chinese art.

[11] 'And in the brouhaha they were dancing the polka.'

[12] Shakespeare, *King Lear* III iv.

III

Because I do not hope for sperm again,[1]
Even the worm has sperm,
Because I do not hope
Desiring this man's God and that man's Pope,[2]
Because I am no Pryce but only Jones,[3]
Because I have no price but only bones,
Can these bones live?[4]
Here there is no seed but only sewing-parties,
I will say Compline, Terce and Nones
In the valley of dead bums.

Nothing is forbidden here, but there is no smoking.
The poplars are felled[5] in the monastery garden
Between the spotted laurels and the rhododendrons.
The monks have departed,
And Princess Marie Louise[6] has gone off with the Abbot.
Come into the shadow of this earth-closet,
And I will show you a packet of woodbines,
Wild woodbines[7] which Willy brought me a week ago.
They call him the buttery boy.

---

[1] 'Because I do not hope to turn again.' T. S. Eliot, *Ash Wednesday*.

[2] 'Desiring this man's gift and that man's scope' (T. S. Eliot, *Ash Wednesday*); cf. 'Desiring this man's art and that man's scope' (Shakespeare, sonnet 29).

[3] A reference to Alan Pryce-Jones (1908–2000), very briefly an Oxford undergraduate (Magdalen 1927–8), then a book and theatre critic, editor, journalist and author.

[4] Ezekiel 37: 3, echoed by Eliot's 'Shall these bones live?' in *Ash Wednesday*.

[5] William Cowper, 'The Poplar Field', 1784. *In a Monastery Garden* (1914) was a well-known piece of descriptive music by Albert Ketelby.

[6] Princess Marie-Louise (1872–1956), a granddaughter of Queen Victoria, active in charitable causes.

[7] A brand of cigarette. 'Woodbine Willie' was the nickname of the Army chaplain and First World War poet the Revd Geoffrey Studdert Kennedy (1883–1929).

Those are girls where stare his eyes.[1]
Nothing of him that is queer
But a mouth that shows white teeth as it broadens
    from ear to ear.

I should like to help him.

Remember now thy Creator
In the days of thy middle age.[2]
Remember now
Remember.
Who has remembered him, who has forgotten?
Sparrow my sister, my sister Sparrow,
How can your parts be full of the spring?[3]
Bats in the belfry calling
Bawd, bawd, bawd.
The tiles are loosened, falling, falling;[4]
Isn't that a nobbly one, quite the latest style?[5]
Where did you get that hat?
John Sparrow and John Sparrow and John Sparrow
To the last syllabub of recorded crime.[6]

---

[1] 'Those are pearls that were his eyes.' T. S. Eliot, *The Waste Land*, quoting Shakespeare, *The Tempest* I ii.

[2] 'Remember now thy Creator in the days of thy youth.' Ecclesiastes 12: 1.

[3] 'Swallow, my sister, O sister swallow, / How can thine heart be full of the spring?' Swinburne, 'Itylus', *Poems and Ballads*, First Series, 1904. For (John) Sparrow see 14/2.

[4] The explanation of what are surely allusions to Bowra's title and subtitle for his poems eludes the editors.

[5] 'Where did you get that hat? [. . .] And isn't it a nobby one, / And what a proper style?' Dundee broadside ballad, 'Where did you get that hat?', c.1880–1900.

[6] 'Tomorrow, and tomorrow, and tomorrow, [. . .] To the last syllable of recorded time.' Shakespeare, *Macbeth* V v.

Queens have died old and fair,
Lust has thinned Hampshire's[1] hair.
Lord, have mercy upon us.[2]

Gaslight and evensong,
And after that the Park,
And may there be no closing of the bar[3]
On a summer evening round behind the doss-house.
Here are the King's Dragoons, the Brazilian sailors.
I fancy a touch of the tar.
When Ernie's boy had the scarlet fever, I said,
Just you let him say if he fancies it.
If he fancies it, that's understood.
For a little of what you fancy does you good.

There's somewhere east of Suez[4]
Where a man can raise a loan.
Cairo, Jerusalem, Alexandria.
The wise men have come to the Shepherds' Hotel.[5]
Are you showing a star in the east?
The foolish virgins have queued up inside
To adjust their dress before leaving.
Send us bright one, light one, hoarhorn,
Quickening and womb-fruit.[6]

---

[1] Stuart Hampshire (1914–2004), Balliol classics 1933–6, philosopher, Fellow
of All Souls 1936–40; at the time of this poem serving in military intelligence;
later held professorships at London and Princeton; Warden of Wadham
1970–84; see also 142/§.

[2] 'Queens have died young and fair; / Dust hath closed Helen's eye; [. . .]
Lord, have mercy on us!' Thomas Nashe, 'In Time of Pestilence', 1593.

[3] 'And may there be no moaning of the bar.' Tennyson, 'Crossing the Bar',
Demeter and Other Poems, 1889.

[4] 'Ship me somewheres east of Suez, where the best is like the worst, /
Where there aren't no Ten Commandments an' a man can raise a thirst.'
Kipling, 'Mandalay', 1892.

[5] Shepherd's [*sic*] Hotel in Old Cairo, favoured by wealthy foreigners.

[6] 'Send us bright one, light one, Horhorn, quickening and wombfruit.'
James Joyce, *Ulysses*, 1922, chapter 14 ad init.

I went to a shop and I asked for a bed,
But the lady said, Bam-bar, the donkey is dead.
Halleluia, mine's a rum.[1]

There was a lady loved a swine,
Spunk, said she.[2]
The crabs are crawling over silent knees.
βλῶσκω, μολοῦμαι, ἔμολον, μέμβλωκα,[3]
Drip, drop, drip, drop, drop, drop, drop.
   Clap. Clap. Clap.

4 April 1941

[1] Inspired by the 1933 Al Jolson film *Hallelujah I'm a Bum*.

[2] 'There was a lady loved a swine; / Honey, quoth she, / Pig-hog, wilt thou be mine? / Hoogh, quoth he.' Nursery rhyme, originally a popular song of the seventeenth century.

[3] Principal parts (present, future, aorist, perfect) of an irregular Greek verb: *blōskō, moloumai, emolon, memblōka* ('I am coming', 'I shall come', 'I came', 'I have come').

Milord

Milord[1] struts over the golfing green;
    He swings his cleek in the air.
Red streamers frisk from his gartered legs,
    And crisp is his curling hair.
As he gallantly waves his eyeglass round,
    Luxurious visions his spirit fill
Of Giton, Kim, Alesha, Bobs,[2]
    To hold him close and very still.

Milord's sweet accents entrance the court.
    With wit he expounds the laws.
He moves all hearts and cajoles the judge,
    And thunderous is the applause.
Of all the high-born ladies there
    The loveliest awaits his will;
His Duchess[3] opens her marble arms
    To hold him close and very still.

---

[1] Cyril Radcliffe (18/3), from one of whose youthful compositions ('The Aristocrat', in *Spring's Highway: Being poems written between the ages of 14 and 19*, 1919) this poem is derived. In 1941 Radcliffe had temporarily abandoned his highly successful career at the Chancery bar to serve in the Ministry of Information, subsequently being appointed its Director-General; his role as a leading public servant lay ahead.

[2] The bearers of these nicknames remain unidentified. Giton was the young slave-boy in Petronius' *Satyricon* (1st century AD), for whose favours the narrator and his friend compete. Kim is the boy hero of Kipling's eponymous novel (1901). Alesha perhaps refers to the youngest of the Karamazov brothers in Dostoevsky's 1879 novel. The most famous 'Bobs' – immortalised by Kipling in his *Barrack-Room Ballads and Other Verses* (47/§) – was Field-Marshal Lord Roberts of Kandahar (1832–1914), but the nickname was presumably common amongst other bearers of the same surname.

[3] In 1939 Radcliffe had married Antonia Tennant (1903–82), née Benson, daughter of 1st Baron Charnwood.

Milord is king of the Money Mart
    And rules what is bought or sold.
Choice paintings[1] hang from his scutcheoned walls,
    And his teeth are filled with gold.
Down the sunny roads of his well-loved France
    He rides in a Rolls and foots the bill.
In the Ritz Hotel is an onyx bath
    To hold him close and very still.

Milord is sunk in a deathly grief;
    He bows his comely head.
He knows his cash and his credit gone;
    His world and his day are dead.
The gilded salons are closed to him.
    His mother,[2] poor sweet, is worn and ill;
For the gaoler has taken his brother Ralph[3]
    To hold him close and very still.

Milord in the gloaming takes his ease;
    He hears his bloodhound bay,
And throned on a yellow pouf he enjoys
    The end of a perfect day.
Here is no labour, here no blush,
    No lips that lust and no eyes that kill.
A corpse is laid in the bridal bed
    To hold him close and very still.

15 April 1941

---

[1] Radcliffe was a noted connoisseur of the arts, and assembled a collection of impressionist paintings.

[2] Sybil Radcliffe, née Cunliffe, described by Cyril Radcliffe's biographer as 'talented and artistic and ambitious for her children [. . .] the driving force in the family'. Edmund Heward, *The Great and the Good: A Life of Lord Radcliffe*, 1994, 5.

[3] Radcliffe's younger brother Ralph (1905–74), Magdalen history 1924–7, antiques-seller. The misfortune that allegedly befell the Radcliffe family has either been well concealed or, perhaps more probably, resulted from Bowra's talent for making a fictional mountain out of a genuine molehill.

Sylvester and Pauline

Sylvester was a blithesome boy,[1]
His parents' pride, his usher's[2] joy;
    All gave him their applause,
Amazed that one so young could speak
In unknown tongues, decipher Greek
    And grasp Dame Nature's laws.

§ This poem appears to have been written specifically for the pleasure of its subjects, since Bowra immediately sent it to Sylvester Gates (6/1), humorously alleging that in a mid-Victorian anthology he had found 'a poem whose moral purpose can hardly fail to interest you and your charming wife [. . .]. It seems to derive from some pupil of dear old William Wordsworth or at least of some poet from the group which, in my humble opinion at least, is inaptly termed the Lake School' (letter dated 8 May [1941] from Bowra to Sylvester Gates).

John Sparrow commented that this poem is 'fiction from beginning to end', and for those who knew the subjects, much of the humour would certainly have sprung from the distortion of real life. But there is a kernel of truth, as the central incident of the poem is based on a real event. Sylvester and Pauline Gates went to New York on their honeymoon in 1936. While there they dined with Bowra at 21 (named from its location at 21 West 52nd Street), then as now one of New York's most prestigious restaurants. After a first course of oysters, a waiter upset a soup tureen over Pauline and, in fury, Sylvester flung over the table. (The party then left, Bowra exclaiming 'Splendid, splendid! We have had a first course free so let's go on elsewhere!')

Although Bowra acknowledges Sylvester Gates's calm exterior (*Memories*, 197), Gates was notorious for his temper: according to Henry Yorke's son Sebastian, he was 'irascible, a complainer about wine. He was said to have hit a man on the head with his own wooden leg' (*Romancing* [xxviii/3], 322). Gates had a brilliant academic career at Winchester College and New College, studied international law at Harvard, and practised as a barrister before turning to public service and banking. His wife Pauline (1907–68) came from a more Bohemian background: her father was the painter Algernon Newton RA, her brother the actor Robert Newton (118/4), and when she became Gates's second wife in 1936 she already had two children by her first husband, Basil Murray, the wild journalist son of Professor Gilbert Murray and his wife Mary (87/§); Basil died in the Spanish Civil War in 1937.

[1] Cf. 'Augustus was a chubby lad; / Fat ruddy cheeks Augustus had.' English translation of Heinrich Hoffmann, 'Die Geschichte vom Suppen-Kaspar' ('The story of Augustus who would not have any soup') in *Der Struwwelpeter* (40/5).

[2] An archaic term, still used in some public schools, for an assistant schoolmaster.

In the dim library at home
His eager spirit learned to roam
    On mountains of the mind
With Martin Tupper, Samuel Smiles[1]
And every master who beguiles
    The spirit unconfined.

On Sundays after Matins he
Would walk with grave solemnity
    In Richmond Park or Kew
And mark the araucaria grow
Or see the tropic cactus throw
    Its foliage to the blue.

At sundown when the lamp was lit
On a tall stool he used to sit
    And strike the ivory keys,
Or make his parents' hearts rejoice
With liquid trillings of his voice
    In old-time melodies.

The wiseling child was sent to school
And dutifully kept each rule
    That riper wisdom made;
In classroom, chapel, playing-ground
He passed the customary round
    And sported, worked and played.

---

[1] Martin Tupper (1810–89) published his most famous work, *Proverbial Philosophy*, in a series of volumes between 1838 and 1867, and *Self-Help* by Samuel Smiles (1812–1904) appeared in 1859. Both books are full of moral exhortations to self-improvement and were great successes with the Victorian reading public.

But ah! what human tongue can say
What flaws lurk hid in human clay
    And mar the finest mould?
The smallest fault unchecked may grow
To work the spirit's overthrow
    And lead to harm untold.

Anger that ill becomes our kind,
Unbalancing the sober mind,
    Was poor Sylvester's bane.
His Seraph face would sweat and shake,
His feet would stamp, his frame would quake,
    Till he seemed scarcely sane.

Sometimes for reason small or none,
If others pulled his hair in fun,
    He kicked and scratched and bit.
Wild lightnings flashing from his eyes
Caused disapproval and surprise;
    His mouth would froth and spit.

One day the post a missive brought
That plunged his father deep in thought
    And turned his hair to white.
The boy, he read, must no more stay
To spoil his comrades' work and play,
    But vanish from their sight.

No need to dwell on what occurred.
His father spoke no hasty word,
    But Christian-like forgave.
He took his boy away from school
And gave him an attorney's stool
    That might his spirit save.

Time passed. December turned to May.
His reverend seniors would say
   How well the young man fared.
From dawn to nightfall he would draw
Up documents of subtle law
   Till none with him compared.

On Saturday when work was done
He brought what shillings he had won
   His parents' hearts to cheer.
No cloud obscured that summer sky,
No prophet raised his voice to cry
   That ruin hovered near.

As yet, it hapt, Sylvester's gaze
Had never turned with wild amaze
   Upon the fairer sex.
No sudden yearnings seized his soul;
He had not seen the aureole
   That womankind bedecks.

On Richmond Hill he chanced to see
A maiden whose sweet modesty
   Outshone all costlier grace,
And on the paving-stone he stood
Stiff as an image made of wood
   That's fastened to its place.

The breath of violets in her hair
Was an enchantment past compare;
   Her figure like a boy's,
Her neat but elegant attire
Flooded his spirit with desire
   To make her share his joys.

His passion was not unreturned.
In her too hope and longing burned
    To taste of nuptial bliss;
And soon they fixed a wedding-day
When both should walk in fine array
    And Pauline should be his.

The rites were done, the knot was tied;
And then the bridegroom and his bride
    The bond would celebrate,
Not with lascivious song and dance
But with true Christian circumstance
    And gaiety sedate.

A humble ale-house, clean and neat,
They chose to take their ritual meat
    And drink their ritual beer,
Their only guest the clergyman
Who blessed their holy union
    Though sunk into the sere.

But who could tell that, when the three
Sat down to celebrate their glee,
    Something was much amiss,
That fires long dead would flame again
And in much agony and pain
    Obliterate their bliss?

The host brought up the bridal cake
And cut it so that each could take
    A piece and have a wish.
Unsteadily he carried it;
He dropped the load and chanced to hit
    Sweet Pauline with the dish.

Black wrath rose to Sylvester's head;
He wished the clumsy fellow dead,
     And plainly told him so.
'My wife is monstrously misused;
Her shapely legs are black and bruised.
     Out, or I'll make you go.'

The host, though not inclined to pride,
The ill-considered charge denied.
     'We are no lackeys here.
Come, come, sir, this is not the way
To treat us. Leave the tavern, pray.
     No word I wish to hear.'

The kind old parson wished to leave;
He loathed to see the good man grieve,
     And hid behind the door.
A deathly pallor seized Pauline;
She could not bear the painful scene
     And swooned upon the floor.

But anger can make mad the wise,
And battle in Sylvester's eyes
     Shone like a levin-brand.[1]
Like an infuriate bull at bay
He snorted, rushed into the fray,
     And struck with either hand.

The table where they sat to sup
Without ado he lifted up;
     With all its glass and plate
He sent it hurtling through the air,
And after it he flung a chair
     That struck the keeper's pate.

---

[1] Thunderbolt.

With fierce artillery of corks,
Dish-covers, ladles, spoons and forks,
   He carried on the fight.
In deadly certainty of aim
The variegated missiles came
   To vent his savage spite.

The inn-keeper then summoned all
His scullions with resounding call
   To gather round their chief.
The clamour of the battle then
When one man fought a host of men
   Was almost past belief.

The watchmen heard the raucous din
And came inquisitively in
   To see if all was well.
The upturned tables, broken glass,
The bodies in a huddled mass,
   Had their own tale to tell.

Breathless, they saw Sylvester fly
And fall upon an enemy
   And fell him to the ground.
With clawing hands he clutched the head
And beat and banged it till it bled
   And teeth flew all around.

'When such things come to pass,' they cried,
'And anarchy bursts forth in pride,
   The law must claim its own.'
They set the gyves about his hands
And fastened him with hempen bands
   And led him off alone.

Here, reader, I might end my tale.
Sylvester was confined to gaol
    Ten years in Cricklewood.
But He who rules the world decreed
That from this fell and ugly deed
    Should come not ill but good.

For when the prisoner left his bars
And looked, a free man, on the stars,
    New hope was in his breast.
No more he sought to shout and rage,
But wished to spend his riper age
    In peace and pious rest.

Sweet Pauline furthered his desire,
And adding an angelic fire
    And innocence all her own,
Helped on his course of sanctity
Till now, by all commended, he
    Sits on a Bishop's throne.

8 May 1941

The Dying Duke

Get out my red pyjamas and the best black velvet sheet,
And place hot-water bottles at my head and at my feet,
The rubber water-bottles that the Air Chief Marshal sent
With their covers of pink satin and embroidered ornament.

Then boil up six fresh lemons and make some lemonade;
I cannot take the substitutes that are of crystals made.
You say there are no lemons. But the Food Controller should
Know that they're indispensable for convalescent food.

And bring the two thermometers, the large one and the small,
Tho' nothing in the world can make my temperature fall.
And put the small one in my mouth, the large one in my pit,
And please don't breathe upon it when you take a look at it.

My nose has not ceased bleeding, and the blood that flows is
    blue;
It's just because, like royalty, I have a skin too few.
Nurse says that it is bad blood, but she can hardly tell.
She does not even realise that I am far from well.

And please I want an enema to ease my colon pains;
Nurse could implant it easily if she would use her brains.
Then give me my three medicines and add an opium pill.
The new pain in my rectum shows that I am very ill.

§ The speaker is Edward ('Eddy') Sackville-West (1901–65), 5th Baron
Sackville 1962, literary and music critic, translator, biographer, playwright,
novelist and accomplished pianist. A homosexual, he suffered chronic ill-health
all his life, including an inherited complaint which caused frequent copious
nosebleeds; despite constant pain and a masochistic personality, his physical
energy and strong will-power kept him active. He was the inspiration for the
character of Uncle Davey in Nancy Mitford's *The Pursuit of Love*, 1945. The
poem is in the metre of Macaulay's 'The Armada', first published in
*Friendship's Offering; and Winter's Wreath: A Christmas and New Year's Present
for MDCCCXXXIII*, 1833.

I have not slept a wink for weeks and shall not sleep tonight;
The bed is too uncomfortable, the pillows are not right.
The lamp-shade is so vulgar, and dear me, oh this room,
I fear I shall not leave it till I go to my tomb.

Tell Morgan[1] he must write my life and say what must be
    said;
There's none but he to do it now Virginia[2] is dead.
It was most inconsiderate of her to go and die
And leave me no biography to be remembered by.

I want the Gothic chamber where I have lived alone
To be a shrine of memory to all that I have done.
So do not move the mirrors or take down the green glass ball
Or disarrange the tapestries that hang along the wall.

The portraits and the marble busts that have been made of
    me
I want them all exhibited in a great gallery.
Pilgrims will come to visit them and see how artists can
Portray the living image of an English nobleman.

I have not very much to say. My time is getting brief.
But when the end has come for me, break not your hearts in
    grief.
But put some rouge upon my lips, some gold-dust on my hair
Just to remind the world that once I too was young and fair.

And let six all-in wrestlers carry my body round
And lay it out to public view upon the tennis-ground;
'Twas there I had my triumphs, and I seldom lost a game,
Tho' lately my back-handed strokes have hardly been the
    same.

---

[1] E. M(organ) Forster (1879–1970), novelist.
[2] The novelist and critic Virginia Woolf (1882–1941).

Bring out the great piano there, and let Lord Berners[1] write
A special funeral-march for me and play it day and night;
And let the three Cathedral choirs[2] join in the final song,
And let the orchestration be intricate but strong.

Tell Epstein[3] he must carve for me an alabaster tomb,
And place it in the middle of the largest drawing-room.
Let Duncan[4] paint the panels, and let good Henry Moore[5]
Emblazon my escutcheon on the sanctuary door.

I wonder what my friends will do when I am dead and gone.
Tell Billa to devote more time to 'soins de la personne'.[6]
I often wonder if she gets as much fun out of Roy[7]
As years ago he did from me when I was all his joy.

There's no one else to take my place in Kelly and Debrett;
And many of the readers soon will find their eyes are wet.
David[8] must write a summary of me in *Who Was Who*,
And tell of all that I have done and all I tried to do.

---

[1] 29/3.

[2] Gloucester, Hereford and Worcester Cathedral choirs combine for an annual musical festival, held by rotation in the three Cathedrals.

[3] Jacob Epstein (1880–1959), sculptor; his works include Oscar Wilde's tomb.

[4] The artist Duncan Grant (1885–1978).

[5] Henry Moore (1898–1986), abstract sculptor and (naturalistic) war artist, an unusual choice for heraldry; he later illustrated Sackville-West's *The Rescue*, 1946.

[6] 'Attention to personal appearance'.

[7] Billa and Roy Harrod (34/3).

[8] Probably Lord David Cecil (1902–86), Fellow of Wadham 1924–30 and of New College 1939–69; Goldsmiths' Professor of English Literature, Oxford, 1948–69.

Many will miss me sadly when I have passed beyond,
Helen,[1] and Sibyl Colefax,[2] and dearest Rosamond.[3]
I cannot think what Jane will do left all alone with K[4]
Without me to support her throughout the livelong day.

Perhaps I've lived too much for love and flung away my heart
To anyone who needed it. It was the better part.
I know I gave them pleasure, and I think I did them good
By showing that one heart was kind that beat with Norman
     blood.

I know that jealous tongues complain that oft I led them on,
But all I did was done for them and brought me little fun.
But my cheeks have lost their crimson and my hair's no
     longer gold,
And few today remember what charms I had of old.

My asthma has come on again. The end is very near,
And to my failing eyesight new worlds of bliss appear.
A coronet awaits me there as bright as this on earth,
And I shall sit in glory with the souls of noblest birth.

Oh dear, I had forgotten, there's a concert on at eight,
And if I am not up at once, I fear I shall be late.
I can't afford to miss it – it would cause too great distress.
So please call for a taxi and put out my evening-dress.

16 July 1941

---

[1] Lady Dashwood (1899–1989), née Helen Eaton, chatelaine of West
Wycombe Park, Buckinghamshire. Her many regular weekend guests during
the war included Nancy Mitford and Sackville-West, who 'used to come down
to dinner every evening wearing a long, blue velvet cloak fastened round the
neck with a silver buckle, and his place at the table was festooned with tiny
snuff boxes crammed with pills[, which] he consumed at intervals throughout
the meal'. Michael De-la-Noy, *Eddy: The Life of Edward Sackville-West*, 1999, 182.
[2] The professional name of Lady Colefax (1874–1950), society hostess and
interior designer.
[3] The novelist Rosamond Lehmann (112/§).
[4] Jane and Kenneth Clark (13/3, 13/2).

The Statesman's Tragedy

To Westminster they voted me,
  They voted me;
And cheers rang loud in ecstasy
  When I rose on the floor.
I spoke on many an act and bill;
I voiced the starving people's will,
And elder statesmen sat quite still
  And begged me to speak more.

The kingdom knew my beck and call,
  My beck and call.
My word was hearkened to by all;
  For all men held me dear.
I kept his secrets for the King
Who told me all and every thing;
And solemn ministers would bring
  Their troubles to my ear.

---

§ This parody of Thomas Hardy's 'The Trampwoman's Tragedy' (in *Time's Laughingstocks and Other Verses*, 1909) blends fact and fiction in its account of the triangular relationship between the publisher and Conservative politician (and future Prime Minister) Harold Macmillan (1894–1986), his wife Lady Dorothy Macmillan (1900–66), née Cavendish, daughter of the 9th Duke of Devonshire, and her long-time lover, the charismatic bisexual Conservative politician Robert Boothby (1900–86). In reality the affair between Boothby and Dorothy was indeed driven by her sexual passion for him; Macmillan and Boothby were political colleagues and remained friends despite the affair; and in 1941 Boothby, a rising political star, was forced to resign from his post as Parliamentary Secretary at the Ministry of Food when a parliamentary enquiry found that he had acted improperly in pressing for the compensation of Czech citizens for lost assets without revealing that he had a financial interest in the success of one such claim, made by a lady and her two daughters. But the supposed financial bargain between Macmillan and Boothby, the suggestion that Macmillan exposed Boothby, and the melodrama of Boothby's fall from power all spring from Bowra's fertile imagination.

[75]

My days were spent in gilded state,
    In gilded state.
I ate off gold and silver plate,
    And drank the choicest wine.
High ladies bent their gaze on me;
They thought me all a man should be;
For never had they dreamed to see
    Such manhood as was mine.

And little chaps with tender eyes,
    With tender eyes,
Would gape on me in mad surprise,
    And stroke my thick black hair,
Or seated on an eiderdown
Would fumble with my dressing-gown,
And turn on me a puzzled frown
    Or little loving stare.

From Romney Marsh to Orkney Isle,
    To Orkney Isle,
All knew and loved my winsome smile.
    I was their fancy-man.
In herring-fleets and beetroot-farms
They longed to nestle in my arms.
There had not been such melting charms
    Since history began.

A duke's daughter was driven mad,
    Was driven mad,
By the soft winning ways I had.
    She thought of none but me.
From husband and from marriage-bed
She shrank in horror and in dread.
She sighed to win my lustihead
    And manly potency.

She begged me oft with tears of grief,
    With tears of grief,
To grant her misery relief
    And take her to be mine.
Such love was never known before;
She lay and grovelled on the floor.
Without me she could live no more.
    She 'gan to peak and pine.

Deeply I felt the pang of it,
    The pang of it.
Upon my bed I made her sit;
    I brushed her tears away,
And with a pitying embrace
I laid her in my sleeping-place;
She was a girl of ducal race.
    I could not say her nay.

I kissed her as she begged me to,
    She begged me to.
It was the least that I could do.
    I settled at her side.
She gasped with joy to win her prize,
To have one of such strength and size
With coal-black hair and coal-black eyes
    In all his power and pride.

So softly passed the nights and days,
    The nights and days.
And yet her goodman turned his gaze
    From what I did for her.
Her hapless husband, whiskered Hal,[1]
Would gaily greet me in the Mall
As tho' I were his truest pal
    And no adulterer.

---

[1] Harold Macmillan.

But whiskered Hal, that loveless man,
   That loveless man,
Conceived a stealthy secret plan
   To mitigate his gloom.
With crafty words and subtle wile,
With double face and jaunty smile,
He set about him to beguile
   Me to an ugly doom.

In friendly guise he came to me,
   He came to me.
He said: 'A duke's daughter is she,
   And she is mad for you.
But still she bears an ancient name,
And I must keep her storied fame
From blot of scandal or of shame;
   The world must deem her true.

'Her love for you I understand,
   I understand.
The little price that I demand
   Is set out in this deed.
Give me five thousand pounds a year,
And you shall have my dearest dear.
Come sign your name and have no fear.
   The woman shall be freed.'

I signed along the dotted line,
   The dotted line.
I did it for her sake, not mine.
   Oh, she was mad for me.
I yielded to her man's device.
For her I made the sacrifice.
Tho' burdensome indeed the price
   I felt it had to be.

I had to get five thousand pounds,
   Five thousand pounds;

[78]

And dismally I went my rounds
　　To find what I could find.
I visited my dearest friend,
A man with stores of wealth to spend,
And begged his charity to lend
　　The gold to ease my mind.

'Of scrip and gold I have no store,
　　I have no store.
What once was mine is mine no more,
　　But spent on dance and song.
My mistresses have swallowed all;
I have no friend on whom to call;
I cannot find the wherewithal
　　To help myself along.

'But orphans three are in my care,
　　Are in my care;
They have good money and to spare.
　　Of this you may partake.
'Twill bring you freedom from your cares.
No man shall know that it is theirs.
Let us divide in equal shares.
　　It is a gallant stake.'

He showed it me, the good Czech gold,
　　The good Czech gold,
And through my hands the pieces rolled.
　　They set my heart astir.
Content in sooth was I to see
The cash that set my lady free
From impotence and slavery.
　　I thought of none but her.

But whiskered Hal, the double-dyed,
　　The double-dyed,
The squalid-souled and serpent-eyed,
　　Knew whence the money came.

He found the orphans in the street
Begging for scraps of bread or meat.
His words were soft, his smile was sweet;
  He played a crafty game.

In brutish rage they told him all,
  They told him all.
With tears they conjured him to call
  The law to help their need.
In hypocritic wrath he swore
To get them back their gold and more;
He was the guardian of the poor,
  And he would act with speed.

Six officers in weaponed state,
  In weaponed state,
Went marching forth that evening late
  To make a fell arrest.
They caught my best friend in his bed
With mistresses at foot and head;
They pricked his buttocks till they bled
  And truncheoned him with zest.

They carted him to Brixton Gaol,
  To Brixton Gaol.
His heart began to quake and quail;
  His face turned green and blue.
And when the rack was carried in,
He only sought to save his skin
And shameful liberty to win
  By telling all he knew.

They hunted me both near and far,
  Both near and far.
They found me in a liquor-bar.
  I fought them till they fell.
I left three officers for dead,
And through the darkened streets I fled.

There was a price upon my head,
    But life I would not sell.

Gray councillors of Church and State,
    Of Church and State,
In solemn conclave held debate
    On what price I must pay.
They seized my mansions and my lands,
And drunken judges gave commands
To grab my lady with rough hands
    And force her to lewd play.

His Majesty had been my friend,
    Had been my friend,
But he betrayed me in the end.
    My name he spoke no more.
His lips were sealed, his tongue was tied;
His old acquaintance he denied;
With his own hands a noose he tied
    To swing me from his door.

I tricked them all. I cut my hair,
    I cut my hair,
And now a redcoat's garb I wear
    And guard a barracks' gate.
And those who jest and quaff with me
Have little thought that one they see
So modest in their company
    Once moved among the great.

But when at night I toss awake,
    I toss awake,
I meditate the toll I'll take
    Of Hal the shifty-eyed.
Though I live now in direful need,
Before me paths of honour lead,
And I shall make that cuckold bleed
    And glut my wounded pride.

5 January 1942

[81]

A Young Man and Old

All the world and that old Prof.
Are not worth the thinking of
For a lad who overmuch
Loves to try the Nelson touch.
Every worm becomes a rod
On the wide seas under God.
    A square peg in a round hole.

Engines rattle at the door;
Mouth must do what shanks abhor.
Did not sage Plotinus say
Every bitch must have her day?
I have slept on floors enough
Not to shrink if skins are rough.
    A square peg in a round hole.

Seamen undischarged will find
Misery of brawn and mind.
Every Jack must splash his tar
Till he poke a door ajar.
But a bowline on a bite
Makes the cock scream in delight.
    A square peg in a round hole.

---

[1] This sequence of verses parodies the poetry of W. B. Yeats, particularly 'A Woman Young and Old' and 'Words for Music Perhaps', both in *The Winding Stair and Other Poems*, 1933. Whether the first three sections refer to specific individuals or to fictional archetypes is not clear, except that 'Prof.' is clearly Dr Zaehner (29/§).

All that I crave is a mouthful of joy
  (Said the squalid pallid soldier lad);
Be it a man or be it a boy,
To me he is better than Helen of Troy.

The moon's gone down and the lamps are out
  (Said the reckless feckless travelling man),
And tho' you are but an ugly lout,
There is swill in your trough to feed my snout.

Oh do it to me and do it again
  (Said the squalid pallid soldier lad);
This unicorn brings such ravishing pain,
I could ride on it till the big stars wane.

The wick's burnt down and the tallow spilt
  (Said the reckless feckless travelling man),
And the stink is foul on the red rep quilt;
But I'll do it again till I make you wilt.

III

You tell me that I prink and preen
   Before the looking-glass,
As if I were a raddled queen
   Who is not what she was.
Mine is the worst of all bad names,
   And good men are estranged.
I'm thinking of the shape I had
   Before my sex was changed.

What if I comb my yellow hair
   Or speak a trifle high,
Or cast a bold undressing stare
   When shop-boys saunter by?

Upon my dark proclivities
  All appetites have ranged.
I'm thinking of the lads I had
  Before my sex was changed.

IV[1]

The circle of the Zodiac
  Pulls on me from afar,
And I would find companionship
  Where the Twelve Sages[2] are
On gyring pinnacles of thought
  Alone with Dr Parr.[3]

Profound Goronwy[4] thought it out
  That on the farthest star,
Where Farquharson[5] lives out his dream
  In timeless avatar,
The bobbins of the world go round
  Alone with Dr Parr.

Von Hügel[6] heard the legend told
  By wise budgerigar
That on Ben Adams'[7] holy mount

---

[1] The speaker is John Sparrow (14/2).

[2] The College of Twelve Sages, part of the complex system of government in 13th-century Florence, is reflected in the twelve sages encountered by Dante and Beatrice at the end of *Paradiso*, who are transformed into a cosmic clock.

[3] Samuel Parr (1747–1825), schoolmaster, cleric, Latin scholar, committed Whig and political pamphleteer; one of John Sparrow's intellectual passions.

[4] Goronwy Rees (1909–79), journalist and novelist; Fellow of All Souls 1931–46; not noted for profundity.

[5] A(rthur) S. L. Farquharson (1871–1942), philosopher, Fellow and Tutor of Univ. 1899–1942.

[6] Baron Friedrich von Hügel (1852–1925), Modernist Catholic theologian who taught the importance of mysticism; friend of Yeats.

[7] Perhaps a dual reference to 'bare Ben Bulben's head' from W. B. Yeats, 'Under Ben Bulben', *Last Poems*, 1939, and to George Adams (1874–1966), Warden of All Souls 1933–45.

No wind of thought can mar
Such flow of sweetness as I find
Alone with Dr Parr.

v

I learned this at my grammar-school
   (Said the great rogue, Goronwy Rees),[1]
That no one but a saint or fool
   Will fling a woman off his knees.
For women come and women pass,
   And love is always back to start.
One lass is but another lass
   And there is no death of the heart.[2]

With that the sages disagree
   (Said the old beggar, crazy John);
What of the proud affinity
   That Plato meditated on,
When lover and belov'd are bound
   In single consummating fire,
And Kings and Queens go jigging round
   And circle up the climbing spire?

The finest rose in all the world[3]
   (Said the great rogue, Goronwy Rees)
Into a filthy ditch I hurled;
   For love will frolic as you please.

---

[1] 84/4.
[2] Elizabeth Bowen's 1938 novel *The Death of the Heart* is based on events
in 1936, when Goronwy Rees, with whom she was in love, started an affair
with novelist Rosamond Lehmann (112/§) during a house-party at the
Bowen family home in Ireland.
[3] Rosamond Lehmann. Her relationship with Rees came to an abrupt end
in 1940 when she saw a newspaper announcement of his impending
marriage to another woman.

But after that was nothing sweet;
   There was a fever in my blood
Until a young girl's dancing feet
   Have drowned me in a summer flood.[1]

Oh, sense and poetry agree
   (Said the old beggar, crazy John)
That wise men find satiety
   In myriad beauties that are one.
When strangers' bodies come to grips
   In rivalry of thew and thigh,
Familiar savours bruise their lips
And the old porker sniffs the sty.

---

[1] Rees's first novel was entitled *The Summer Flood* (1932).

Gilbert and Mary: an Eclogue

MARY   Gilbert, I wish to have a word with you.
Now don't pretend that you have work to do.
Last week an amorous jaunt of yours was seen
And told me by none other than Pauline.[1]
When watching from her humble upper floor –
You know she can't afford to pay for more –
She saw you carrying a flask of port
And visiting a place of low resort.
A creature with blonde hair and scarlet nails
Answered the door, and oh, description fails
To tell how you planted a shameless kiss
Upon the red lips of the raddled miss.
Enfolded in her arms you went within
And disappeared into the haunt of sin.
What happened afterwards I can but guess.
Now tell the whole truth, neither more nor less.

GILBERT   A big committee of the LNU[2]
Was meeting to discuss what we could do

---

§ Gilbert Murray (1866–1957), Regius Professor of Greek, Oxford, 1908–36, had been Bowra's tutor, and had helped secure him his Fellowship at Wadham. Australian-born, Liberal in politics, an advocate of votes for women, a committed internationalist and a religious agnostic, he was the original of Adolphus Cusins in Shaw's *Major Barbara*. Although tolerant in many ways, Murray was 'rather strait-laced on personal morals' (*Memories*, 225). His wife, Lady Mary Murray (1865–1956), née Howard, daughter of the 9th Earl of Carlisle, was teetotal, vegetarian, in later life a Quaker, and her left-wing sympathies exceeded those of her husband. Unconcerned about her personal appearance, she lacked a sense of humour and Bowra admitted that '[w]ith all her warmth and generosity she could be both bossy and censorious' (*Memories*, 222). Gilbert Murray's many translations of Greek drama and poetry into the style of Victorian poets such as Swinburne gave renewed popularity to Greek literature, but were criticised for their combination of the pedestrian and the overblown: this poem parodies both these characteristics.

[1] Pauline Gates (63/§), formerly the Murrays' daughter-in-law.
[2] The League of Nations Union, founded by Murray and committed to furthering the aims of the League of Nations, was the most important organisation in the British peace movement between the wars.

	To help Assyrian liberals[1] to go
	To Madagascar or Fernando Po.
	Beneš[2] was in the chair and told a tale
	How Masaryk[3] drank too much audit ale;[4]
	He tipsily believed himself a rat
	And called out loudly 'Now bring out your cat!'
MARY	What a dis-gus-ting story! Don't deny
	That you were in the King's Road on the sly.
	I can imagine what a scene took place
	Between you and the little brazen-face.
	Was it the one I sent away from here
	Because I found you whispering in her ear,
	Or is it some new hussy you have found
	Riding in buses or the Underground?
GILBERT	Oft at the summer solstice, it is said,
	Has a wild maiden lost her maidenhead,
	Raped by lewd lovers on a mountain-side.
	In time, of course, she would be deified
	For having borne a pair of heavenly twins.
	The ritual *gamos*[5] of the year begins
	When the all-Father puts on phallic state
	And offers up his member on a plate.
MARY	Gilbert, if you refuse to tell me right,
	I shall cut off your Horlicks from tonight.
GILBERT	I think that I remember what you mean.
	I had to write a leader for the *Queen*[6]

[1] '[Murray] devoted much time and trouble to the Assyrian Christians when they were harried by new masters in the Middle East.' *Memories*, 226.

[2] Edvard Beneš (1884–1948), President of Czechoslovakia 1935–8 (and again after the war).

[3] Tomáš Masaryk (1850–1937), philosopher who became the first President of Czechoslovakia 1918–35; a teetotaller.

[4] Strong ale, originally specially brewed for audit days at certain Oxford colleges.

[5] 'Marriage'.

[6] A society magazine (now part of *Harpers & Queen*).

On classical studies in the Eskimos;
And that was the occasion, I suppose.
In the King's Road a learned lady lives
Who does research on Greek preventatives.
I thought that she might help me to collect
Some details on a queer religious sect
Who think that seminal fluid is the soul
And hang up foreskins on a totem pole.
They make blood-offerings to a pubic rose
And in the goat-dance free their mana[1] flows.
Perhaps it was with her I spent the night;
She does it quietly, and does it right.[2]

MARY   Nonsense. That silly story won't explain
Why your wool muffler has a scarlet stain
Of lipstick and your new black hat presents
Stale odours of disgusting foreign scents.
You know quite well you visited this place
Simply to see a pretty empty face.

GILBERT   I may have dramatised it in my mind.[3]
My recollection is I went to find
Wild honey and the East and loveliness.[4]
She was reciting in a satin dress
Some version that I wrote for her, a thing
Full of sharp anguish and old suffering.

---

[1] 'Spiritual power'.

[2] Murray once commented on a pupil's Greek composition: 'He does it quickly and does it right.'

[3] 'Gilbert was deeply attached to Lady Mary [. . .] but he could not refrain from making mild fun of her. After going to official dinners in London he would, to her horror, regale her with accounts of the huge joints and the lavish alcohol which had been served. Once, when he told a particularly amusing story, she said, "That's not true, Gilbert", and[,] with a charming smile, he answered "I may have dramatised it in my mind", and proceeded to tell another.' *Memories*, 223.

[4] Murray's translation of Aristophanes, *Wasps*, 220.

(*recites*)   Few and far, far and few,[1]
    Words of a whirling daughter,
A wet wild sheet and a flowing sea,[2]
And a blossom of virgin modesty
That opes its lips when the blade strikes true
    And flows with the flowing water.

Few and far, far and few,
    A stroke from a spear-shaft falling
Brings back the dreams of the days that were,
The languid lips and the flowerlike hair,
The limbs that gleam like the falling dew
    And a voice in the midnight calling.

Awake, O my feet, awake,
    With glitter of trembling toes.
      Let the lithe long fingers rove
      On the bosky Mount of Love,
    Where the wild wan insect goes
And the fur is soft in the brake.

Hymen, O Hymen pale,
    Yield to the bold attack.
      Let the taut bowstring snap
      To the roar of a thunderclap
    When the beast lies down on its back
And the bites and the wrestlings fail.[3]

MARY   Your melody recalls the days of old,
        The apple-juice, the peanuts and the cold,

---

[1] Cf. 'Far and few, far and few, / Are the lands where the Jumblies live.' Edward Lear, 'The Jumblies', *Nonsense Songs, Stories, Botany and Alphabets*, 1871.
[2] Among Allan Cunningham's *The Songs of Scotland, Ancient and Modern*, 1825, was his own 'A Wet Sheet and a Flowing Sea', a vigorous sea-ballad.
[3] The previous six lines satirise Murray's translation of Sophocles, *Women of Trachis*, 517–22.

And that so nameless and so shining thing
That made us sick for love and love-making.
You would hold speeches upon women's rights
And bid the children gather round at nights
For tenants' pudding and warm lemonade.
Good Dr Zavitz[1] often with us stayed
And lectured to the Meeting of the Friends.
Then you translated *Where the Rainbow Ends*[2]
Into Greek verse. They often acted it,
And good Jane Harrison[3] watched it from the pit.
Oh far-off happy days of minstrelsy!
Greek for the Greekless, Oh abide with me![4]
Come, let us see if we cannot restore
Some blissful moment of the days of yore.
You shall not find, for all that you have said,
Death and a cold white thing within the bed.[5]
Oh tender twining arms, and Oh the sweet
Falling asleep together in the heat!
Our fate is calling – let us follow quick.
GILBERT   Mary, you've mixed the Horlicks much too thick.[6]

12 July 1941

---

[1] Probably Charles Zavitz (1863–1942), Canadian agriculturalist and Quaker.

[2] A Christmas play for children by Clifford Mills and John Ramsey (1911).

[3] Jane Harrison (1850–1928), classical scholar, Fellow and Lecturer in Classical Archaeology, Newnham, Cambridge, from 1898; often referred to by her contemporaries as 'the cleverest woman in England'.

[4] Cf. 'Help of the helpless, / Oh, abide with me.' Henry Lyte, 'Abide with me', 1847.

[5] Murray's translations were sometimes criticised for his additions to the Greek original. 'A story, apocryphal indeed, but not fundamentally false, tells that in a lecture Murray, on reaching the crisis of the play, said "I will read you my version, 'Death, and a cold white thing within the house . . .' " but those who followed in the Greek found no more than the emotive cries *e e à à*.' *Memories*, 218.

[6] 'The sadder side of their economy was revealed when Gilbert, before going to bed, said in a plaintive voice, "Mary, you've mixed the Horlicks too thick." ' *Memories*, 222.

Song

Ah, but she[1] is very grand,
And her blood is quite quite blue.[2]
Norfolk and Northumberland
Bless the bank[3] on which she grew.
County families display
Gurneys, Gurneys all the way.[4]

She could never set an end
To her territorial claims.
Vainly Herts and Beds contend
That they boast of nobler names.
Every heart and every bed
Know a lass unparalleled.

Every decent Oxford dame,
Mrs Taylor,[5] Mrs Lowe,[6]
Make obeisance to her name,
Praise it to all winds that blow.
Nanny Cecil[7] knows her place,
Drops a curtsey to her grace.

§ A parody of Shakespeare's song 'Take, O take those lips away', *Measure for Measure* IV i.

[1] Billa Harrod (34/3).

[2] Cf. 'What wonderfully blue eyes you have, Ernest. They are quite, quite blue.' Oscar Wilde, *The Importance of Being Earnest*, Act I.

[3] Billa Harrod's paternal grandmother was a Gurney from the Norfolk banking family; Gurney's bank (which became Barclays) was a major financial force in the early nineteenth century. Although the Gurney family had northern connections, the link to Northumberland seems to have been invented by Bowra.

[4] Cf. 'It was roses, roses all the way.' Robert Browning, 'The Patriot: An Old Story', in *Men and Women*, 1855.

[5] Perhaps Margaret, née Garrett, wife of the Revd John Taylor, Principal of Wycliffe Hall, Oxford, 1932–42, Bishop of Sodor and Man 1942–54.

[6] Ruth Lowe, née Burpee, wife of the Dean of Christ Church (138/§).

[7] Presumably Lord David Cecil's wife Rachel (1909–82), daughter of critic Desmond MacCarthy.

Though the roses are most red,
Redder, redder are her lips.
'Twas no common couple bred
Such round legs on such square hips.[1]
Hear the fainting lovers say,
'Take, O take those hips away!'

Crawling round and crawling up,
Noblest sons of noblest line
Know exactly where to stop;
For their mistress is divine,
And their voices thin and high
'Darling, darling, darling!' cry.

All the finest names that are,
Martyred saints of 18B,[2]
Algy Teck[3] and Mary R[4]
Know the highest when they see
Every well-born man and boy
Share his royalties with Roy.[5]

16 August 1942

---

[1] 'Women [. . .] have curves and waists; and most women with a sense of
proportion are thankful to hide their legs.' Letter from Billa Harrod in praise
of the New Look in fashion, *The Times*, 14 February 1948, 5.

[2] During the Second World War, Defence Regulation 18B allowed for the
indefinite detention without charge or trial of those considered a possible
threat to national security. It was used most extensively in 1940 when about a
thousand people suspected of Nazi sympathies were detained, including Sir
Oswald Mosley and his wife Diana.

[3] Alexander Cambridge (1874–1957), né Prince Alexander of Teck, 1st and
last Earl of Athlone 1917; army officer; Governor-General of South Africa
1923–31 and Canada 1940–6. The brother of Queen Mary, he was known
within the family as Alge (*sic*, pronounced 'Algy').

[4] 'Mary Regina', Queen Mary (1867–1953), née Princess Victoria Mary
('May') of Teck.

[5] Roy Harrod (34/3).

Russian Cradle-Song

Time for tots to go to bed;
No more traipsing to and fro.
Where's my silly sleepy-head?
Now to bye-bye she must go.
Baby Bob[1] will cry boo-hoo,
Bayu-bayushki-bayu.[2]

Someone's knocking on the pane,
Murmuring 'It's only Slee.'[3]
Tell him not to come again;
He will not be asked to tea.
Merrily we sing Cuckoo.
Bayu-bayushki-bayu.

What does little —[4] want,
Barking in a fearful fright?
If he wants to come, he can't;
He's been turned out for the night.
No more tricks for him to do.
Bayu-bayushki-bayu.

§ This poem recites the husbands and lovers of Bowra's friend Barbara
Hutchinson (1911–89), 'rich, restless, predatory, with a wicked wit and a lethal
sexual magnetism' (Selina Hastings, *Rosamond Lehmann*, 2002, 267).

[1] Robert Boothby (75/§).
[2] Nonsense syllables characteristic of Russian lullabies.
[3] Possibly an aircraftman, according to Isaiah Berlin.
[4] Name omitted for reasons explained in the preface (see p. xiii above).

Xan[1] is scratching at the door,
Rubs his nose along the sill.
Back he comes to ask for more;
He is very green and ill.
He must go back to the Zoo.
Bayu-bayushki-bayu.

What if surly Victor[2] come
Crawling over hill and dale,
Belching smoke from mouth and bum,
Old Tess[3] riding on his tail?
Smack him, and he'll break in two.
Bayu-bayushki-bayu.

Time to put all toys away.
Only Rex,[4] the teddy-bear,
On the eiderdown may stay,
In his bristling coat of hair.
So to bed and bally-hoo.
Bayu-bayushki-bayu.

4 April 1950

---

[1] Alexander ('Xan') Fielding (1918–91), Special Operations Executive (SOE) agent in Crete and France during the Second World War, writer and translator.

[2] Victor Rothschild (1910–90), 3rd Baron Rothschild 1937; zoologist and businessman; intelligence services 1939–45; Director BOAC 1946–58; Assistant Director of Research, Dept of Zoology, Cambridge, 1950–70. He married Barbara Hutchinson in 1933; they were divorced in 1946.

[3] Teresa ('Tess') Mayor (1915–96), who married her former MI5 colleague Victor Rothschild in 1946.

[4] Rex Warner (1905–86), writer and translator, who became Barbara Rothschild's second husband in 1949. This marriage also ended in divorce and Barbara subsequently married her third and last husband, Niko Ghika.

Old Mortality

In his Sulka shirt
And his Charvet tie[1]
Old Mortality
Passes by.

He follows the line
Of his sensitive nose,
And gaily he prances
On pointed toes.

Oh the swing of his hips
And the wave of his hair –
Eternally youthful
And debonair.

What man can compete
With the exquisite taste
Of his swan-like neck
And his wasp-like waist?

He lives for the raptures
Of 'l'art pour l'art'[2]
And thinks everything else
Is a bit *blafard*.[3]

---

§ Here Bowra mocks Raymond Mortimer (40/3), whose somewhat effete
homosexuality is portrayed in the manner of T. S. Eliot's *Old Possum's Book of
Practical Cats* (1939).

[1] The firms of Sulka in New York and Charvet in Paris were among the
most prestigious producers of gentlemen's apparel.

[2] 'Art for art's sake'.

[3] 'Pallid'.

He has discovered,
And lets you know it,
That Shakespeare's a most
Peculiar poet.

From out-of-date notions
He's charmingly free,
And St John of the Cross[1]
Isn't his cup of tea.

When he enters a café,
Surréalistes stare,
Crying 'Allez-vous en,
Affreuse bergère!'[2]

Among civilised people
He knows only the best;
His only true equal
Is Ed Sackville-West.[3]

All beauty enthrals him,
Especially male;
When he sees it, he flaps
Like a leaf in a gale.

When the dusk has descended,
He wanders afar,
And enjoys a gay tussle
With jolly Jack Tar,

---

[1] A Spanish mystic, Christian philosopher and poet (1542–91), the founder of the 'discalced' branch of the Carmelite order of monks, who went barefoot as part of their commitment to monastic poverty.

[2] 'Go away, frightful shepherdess.' These were apparently the words with which 'an eminent French writer' dismissed Mortimer, who was at the time 'artistically arrayed in a long flowing cloak and big floppy panama hat'. A. L. Rowse, *Friends and Contemporaries*, 1989, 57.

[3] 71/§.

Or expounds to stout guardsmen
The claims of Cézanne.
He knows all the ways
Of a man with a man.[1]

Where else in the world
Can such graces be seen?
Our greatest, our only
Philosopher-queen!

16 April 1950

---

[1] Cf. 'The way of a man with a maid', Proverbs 30: 19.

$$[\,.\,.\,.\,]\ ^{1}$$

---

[1] Poem omitted for reasons explained in the preface (see p. xiii above).

Heldengesang

Oh the pangs of seed unsown,
Aches of anguished appetite;
Love, when left to play alone,
Knows not how to stand upright.
Come, O come, O Gabriele,
Rescue poor repressed Noel.[1]

On the Mount of Venus lies
Brynhild, crackling with blue flame,
Opening great Nordic thighs;
Siegfried hears her call his name;
Past the battlements he vaults
In a set of somersaults.

She will never let him slip,
She will hold him fast and firm
When the Cleopatra grip
Closes on the swelling worm.
And the waters of the Rhine
Mingle with the foaming brine.

Randy Yank and bouncing Boche[2]
Know full well what they are at;
He will give her cat for cosh,
She'll reply with cosh for cat.

---

§ This 'heroic song' anticipates the marriage on 30 June 1950 of Gabriele
Ullstein (b. 1921), translator, journalist and critic, to Noel Annan.

[1] 'O come, O come, Emmanuel / And ransom captive Israel', from John
Neale's 1851 translation of a Latin hymn. Noel Annan (1916–2000), Baron
Annan 1965, historian (particularly of political ideas) and academic
administrator; Fellow of King's College, Cambridge, 1944–56, Provost 1956–66;
later Provost of University College, London, and Vice-Chancellor, University of
London.

[2] Annan's mother was American by birth; his bride was the daughter of the
Berlin publisher Louis Ullstein.

So to bed, and flog away
Till their lashes wake the day.

He can push her from the front,
He can push her from behind;
When the arse becomes a cunt,
Soul and body intertwined,
Turning black and turning blue,
Melt in a delicious glue.

Inside out and upside down,
Counter-cockwise all the night,
With a tasty bit of brown
He will put repressions right;
When the body takes control
Parts are equal to the hole.

Shadowed by prodigious tits,
He'll not mark the years go by;
In the forest of her pits
He will curl his limbs and lie
Very soft and very still
By the great tree Yggdrasil.

When the twilit gods are gone
And the dragon in his den
Gnaws Valhalla to the bone,
Lover and beloved will then
Whirl in fast and fierce delight
Through the everlasting night.

3 June 1950

$$[\,.\,.\,.\,]\,^{1}$$

---

[1] Poem omitted for reasons explained in the preface (see p. xiii above).

The Amazon Queen

In the gilded tent
Of the Amazon queen
The stiff snob peacocks
No longer preen,
And the old tom-cat forgets his piles
And ceases to rut on the randy-tiles.

Dim bodies drift
In a zebra light,
Privy parts bloated
Black and white;
And Time, the cynical old giraffe,
Snaps at the moon with a surly laugh.

---

§ Clearly a parody of Edith Sitwell's performance-poem *Façade*, 1922, and overflowing with the distinctive vocabulary that characterises her work, this poem displays a typically Sitwellian concentration on sound rather than meaning which makes its interpretation more than usually challenging. It appears to be a fantasy on Edith Sitwell's literary circle, the Amazon Queen (despite the incongruous sexual imagery) presumably representing Edith Sitwell (1887–1964) herself; Bowra, a friend of hers, had written a pamphlet (*Edith Sitwell*, 1947) on her poetry. The identity of the other characters in the poem is a matter for speculation: candidates might include Edith's brother Osbert (1892–1969), also a poet, for 'the old tom-cat'; Ezra Pound (1885–1972) for the 'red-haired shape', despite the apparent quotation from Poe's 'The Raven' (or is the reference to Verlaine's 'Nevermore'?); curly-haired Dylan Thomas (1914–53), Edith Sitwell's poetic protégé, for the 'nigger-boy'; and T. S. Eliot (6/§), the Missouri-born author of 'Five-Finger Exercises' (*Criterion*, January 1933) and 'The Hippopotamus' (6/§), for the piano-player. Edith Sitwell was notorious for the relish with which she pursued feuds, so there are numerous possibilities for the hostile 'third' in the poem, including F. R. Leavis (1895–1978) and Wyndham Lewis (1882–1957); but perhaps the most likely contender is critic Geoffrey Grigson (1905–85), a persistent denigrator of Edith Sitwell's poetry, who had been involved in a physical confrontation with one of her supporters, Roy Campbell, some months before this poem was written. Readers will doubtless be able to provide alternative explanations.

Like the still-born child
Of a crazy ape,
Drools in the darkness
A red-haired shape,
Greasily,
Queasily,
Muttering,
Fluttering,
Uttering zanily 'Nevermore'
As he scuttles away on the spunk-spread floor.

On the gold state-bed
Lies the Amazon queen.
The hair on her head
Is ultramarine.
Her right big toe
Is indigo,
And Chinese white
In the peony light
Her great domed arse
Blares as bold as brass,
But the ice-floe spreads from the Arctic cold
And freezes the blood in her to gold.

In shrill staccato
Like a tomato
Every pubic hair
Pipes a dissonant air,
And with a shuddering obbligato
Each armpit
Drums to answer it,
Till the ghosts in the guest house stir their bones
And take their places for Death's Paul Jones.

Who is the nigger-boy romping there?
With sunflowers twined in his twisting hair?

Is it some Mowgli
Fished from the Hooghly?
Or namby-pamby
Little black Samby?
With trim deflections
He turns his erections
To trap the twots of the dancing-girls
And fetter them fast with his snapping curls.

Open his breast
And you'll find a stone,
An icicle
And a bit of bone.
Scorpions crawl from it and start
To fix their fangs on a trembling heart.
They lick and lap and nuzzle and numb
The great white soul in a great white bum.

And who is it who makes a sortie
To wake the voice of the pianoforte?
He slaps the keys
Of the ivories
And the sharps and flats all buzz like bees.
With his papagay smile
And his dim trim style
He lures the girls up the garden path
To the black-toothed jaws of the Gates of Death.

Over the prairies
Far and wide,
Clothed in his hippopotamus-hide,
He used to dance till the night winds sighed;
And all the fairies
Tossed their hair
In the amethyst glint of the neon air;
And fat milch-cows in the Gothic dairies

In amorous dream
Sent him curds and cream,
And made him as stiff as the gold parasol
Which a gangster buys for his gilded Moll.

But the heart grows old
And the wind blows cold.
The icy wind, a society surgeon,
Blows with his bag from blue Spitzbergen,
Whips out a knife
And nips the life
That beats in the heart of the summer rose,
And where it goes
Nobody knows.
For there's nothing left
From the wanton theft
But a gaping hole where the wind has hurled
The rose, red rose, rose of all the world.

A third there is
In the shadows lurking,
Shirking,
Girking,
Squelching,
Belching;
The twisted smile on his crafty lips
Is damned by the curse of the moon's eclipse.
Smirking saliva of serpents' hisses
Clicks in the smack of his Judas kisses,
Stealthily,
Wealthily,
Creeping away,
He shrinks and slinks from the light of day,
But well he knows that the wage of sin
Will hold him soon in its sharp-toothed gin.

The weevil crawls
In his dry-rot brain
And sucks his balls
To a death-watch strain.
A grinning ghoul
Gnaws his cunt-stuck tool;
Phantasmagorical voices call
Through the asylum's padded wall,
And the mumble-tumble plod of his speech
Shrills into a parrot's knife-edged screech.

Straw in his hair
He tumbles sprawling,
Calling,
Bawling,
And caterwauling,
And fumbles a pair
Of pink mice crawling.
Into a thousand more they split
And hurtle into the sulphur pit,
Where the bonfires glare
And the glazed eyes stare
At the red-hot forks tossing souls in the air,
While Mrs Mandragora
Sits in Hell's agora,
Waiting, waiting,
In unabating
Lust for the lost souls hurled down there.

The Amazon queen
Takes her platinum crown,
Weaves tiger-lilies
Into a gown.
Her eyes crack with pistol shots of doom,
And Furies flap from the circling room.
Lolling red tongues, the sex-starved pack
Slobber along the cock-cheese track,

Sniffing the scent as an armadillo
Fumbles under a lady's pillow.
Like a scuttling cockroach runs the prey,
But faster the Furies chew their way,
Till black doom calls
And the victim falls –
And nothing is left but his cock and his balls.

The Amazon queen
On her peacock throne
Holds holiday court
Alone, alone.
She tosses commands to the empty air,
But the stars reply that they do not care.
She threatens their bums with the bastinado,
But they laugh in her face with shrill bravado.
Then she puffs and blows
In the mouth of the moon,
And a mad typhoon
Twists and twirls and flows
Through every nation
And constellation,
Till nought can be seen
Of the Amazon queen
But lightnings flashing from blood-lit eyes,
Planets careering in mad surprise,
And the burst of atoms in skidding skies.
The clock strikes Zero in Arctic snows
And the world is changed to a wild, white rose.[1]

17 August 1950

---

[1] Perhaps a reference to Keats's poem 'Meg Merrilies' (*Hood's Magazine*, 1838, under the title 'Old Meg'), whose heroine was 'brave as Margaret Queen / And tall as Amazon' and 'Her wine was dew of the wild white rose'.

The Meringue-Outang

I sauntered with a vacant mind
Beneath a monkey-puzzle tree,
And sweet was my surprise to find
A body swinging over me.
My spirit leapt with joy and sang
To see a great meringue-outang.

From bough to prickly bough it swung,
And daintily with hands and feet
From the forbidden leafage hung
With motions soft as they were sweet;
It wriggled at a wondrous pace
From airy place to airy place.

Its blue and scarlet bottom shone
Like Brighton Rock at Christmastide;
Each breast was like a cherry bun
With gurgling clots of cream inside;
It spread its legs out and its arms,
Displaying all too female charms.

---

§ Bowra dubbed novelist Rosamond Lehmann (1901–90; cf. 74/3) the
Meringue-Outang at about the time when this poem, a parody of
Wordsworth's 'I wandered lonely as a cloud' (*Poems, in Two Volumes*, 1807),
was written. Beautiful and statuesque, Rosamond was an egoist with a warm
but insecure and emotionally demanding nature which often contributed to
the failure of her relationships with men. In January 1950 Rosamond's long-
time lover, poet Cecil Day Lewis, had abandoned both her and his wife Mary
for actress Jill Balcon. Rosamond's reaction to yet another unhappy end to a
relationship was extreme, and even sympathetic friends found her constantly
repeated complaints of ill usage difficult to endure. Bowra was exasperated by
Rosamond's emotional demands, and on one occasion declared to Edith Sitwell
that 'if [Rosamond] had *one* more affair, he was either going into the lunatic
asylum or was going to shoot himself, because he couldn't stand being kept
up all night while R examined her and everybody else's motives': letter from
Edith Sitwell to Philip Caraman, 30 January 1959, quoted in *Rosamond
Lehmann* (94/§), 269.

She picked the nuts upon the tree
And tossed them gaily in the air;
At whom she aimed I could not see,
But little did I ask or care:
The lovely creature charmed me so,
So gay to see, so sweet to know.

She whistled shrilly to her mate,
And much in truth I envied him,
That his alone should be the fate
Of paying court to such a quim.
She whistled once, she whistled twice,
His male attentions to entice.

Then from the tree-top high in air
A male leapt forth and pelted stones,
Which struck her here and struck her there,
Until she burst in tears and groans.
Oh little had she thought her mate
Would bend on her such vicious hate.

Another male peeped forth to whom
She rolled her eyes and blew a kiss;
He pushed his penis through the gloom
And turned his amber-coloured piss
In foaming flood upon her so
That she was drenched from head to toe.

A third came out. She turned to it
And breathed a melancholy sigh;
He let her have a shot of shit
And caught her neatly in the eye.
Much frightened were the little birds
To see that black cascade of turds.

This way and that she looked in dread.
Poor thing, she could not understand,
Till dazed with fear and nearly dead
She slacked her grip and loosed her hand
And with an earthquake's tearing sound
Heavily tumbled to the ground.

Her eyes were wet with salt green tears;
Her face was wracked with hopeless woe.
Oh, never in the waste of years
Had lovely creature suffered so!
It seemed that all the Simian race
Had eased itself upon her face.

Battered and broken on the ground,
Beyond recovery she seemed.
The shades of death were closing round,
And in her dying hour she dreamed:
She dwelt in an eternal spring
Of Paradisal junketing.

She heard the silken voices coo,
She saw the winsome, wheedling eyes,
When youth and beauty came to woo
Her for the glory of her thighs,
Strong males of huge and hairy breed,
Who burst to spread the Simian seed.

She decked her heart up like a cake
With sugar-ice and marzipan;
She gave a piece to each to take,
And when they ate, a shiver ran
So sweetly down her slender spine
That all her blood was turned to wine.

She poured it out for them to drink,
Passed in a crystal loving-cup,
And gave them little time to think:
The moment that they drank it up,
A gay delirium seized them all
Until the night began to fall.

Then she enclosed them on her breast
And fed them with a world of sighs;
Upon their yielding forms she pressed
The load of her enormous thighs,
And high and low across the room
Blue roses floated in the gloom.

She passed, and far beyond the trees
The beautiful meringue-outang
Makes amorous gestures to the breeze
Where once the stars of morning sang,
And then her heart with pleasure fills
And dances with the great gorills.

18 August 1950

Spring Song

Seymour[1] is y-Culmen in,
Lewdly sing Cuckoo!
Fill the bridal bed with gin,
Throw the Queen of Glory[2] in,
Four is better fun than two,
Woogie-woogie-woo.

When the Henry[3] turneth green,
Momma[4] maketh sport.
Round the May-pole trips Pauline,[5]
Hearts and parts acclaim her queen.
Randy playboys sniff and snort,
Living, loving, caught.

---

§ This parody of the thirteenth-century song *Sumer is icumen in* (memorably performed by Bowra and friends at Uffington: see frontispiece) hints at the tangled love-lives and multiple marriages of some of Bowra's London-based friends.

[1] Mark Culme-Seymour (1910–90), New College 1929–30, a friend of Cyril Connolly and Donald Maclean; the second of his four marriages had ended in divorce in 1949.

[2] A name usually given to the Virgin Mary, though here the unidentified bearer of it seems far from virginal. Cf 'Lift up your head, O ye gates; and be ye lift up, ye everlasting doors; and the King of glory shall come in' (Psalms 24: 7), set to music by Handel in his *Messiah* (1742), and partially quoted by D. H. Lawrence in *Lady Chatterley's Lover* (published in Italy in 1928), chapter 14.

[3] Henry Yorke (1905–73), Magdalen 1924–6; industrialist and, under the name of Henry Green, novelist. He had abandoned Oxford in his third year to work in the Birmingham factory of his father's engineering firm, H. Pontifex and Sons, and later became its Managing Director, based in the firm's London office. His novels include *Living* (1929), *Caught* (1943) and *Loving* (1945). He married only once, but had numerous affairs.

[4] Presumably Yorke's mother, the aristocratic Maud (1874–1963), née Wyndham, daughter of the 2nd Baron Leconfield, whose family home was Petworth; described as 'almost as devoted to her sons as to her horses and dogs', *Romancing* (xxviii/3), 8. The sport in question is likely to be fox-hunting.

[5] Pauline Gates (63/§), who had had an affair with Henry Yorke during the War.

[116]

Girls go grinding like green geese[1]
Till the ganders wilt,
And the glory that was Rees[2]
Melts away like candle-grease,
And the gingerbread is guilt
Where the tallow's spilt.

Artifex and Pontifex[3]
Strike up a duet,
Bursting through the bottlenecks
In the froth and foam of sex.
Throats are dry, but love is wet,
Nuzzle, neck and pet.

Alan[4] sterteth after Jen,[5]
Verteth to the goal,
She can put the fizz in men,
Ply the syphon and say When.
What if love is on the dole?[6]
Climb the greasy pole.

---

[1] Pasture-fed geese, traditionally eaten at Michaelmas.

[2] Goronwy Rees (84/4), notorious for his many love affairs; a Director 1946–53 of H. Pontifex and Sons (116/3). Cf. 'the glory that was Greece' (Edgar Allan Poe, 'To Helen', first published in the 1831 edition of *Poems Written in Youth*, revised 1843).

[3] In ancient Rome *artifex*, the creative artist, was the antithesis of the Pontifex, the Chief High Priest, symbol of religious authority (and see previous note).

[4] Alan Ross (1922–2001), poet and travel writer; for many years cricket correspondent of the *Observer*; Editor, *London Magazine*, 1961–2001. He had relationships with, among many others, Cyril Connolly's second wife Barbara Skelton, during her later marriage to George Weidenfeld, and Deirdre Craven, daughter of Den Craig (119/2), who went on to become the third Mrs Connolly.

[5] Jennifer Fry (1916–2003) had married Alan Ross in 1949, after having briefly been part of a *ménage à trois* at Faringdon House, where her first husband, Robert Heber-Percy, lived as the long-term boyfriend of Lord Berners (29/3). Among her many other admirers were Cyril Connolly (19/2) and Henry Yorke (116/3).

[6] Walter Greenwood's 1933 novel *Love on the Dole* had been filmed in 1941.

Go and fetch the master-key,[1]
Put the girls with pup.
Take a dose of gas for tea,
Break the Lys[2] and scuttle free,
Bedding down and bedding up,
Tipple, topple, tup.

Cheyne Walk[3] is falling down,
Ceilings whirl about.
When Sylvester comes to town
Lightnings whistle from his frown,
And the hot bite of his knout
Gobbles lass and lout.

Doom has come to bounding Bob,[4]
Doom to genial Joy.[5]
Though the children scream and sob,
Though the lover wipes his knob,
Vengeance summons to destroy,
Crying 'Shit ahoy!'

---

[1] Possibly a reference to Robert Kee (b. 1919), author, journalist and
broadcaster, who had shared a house with Cyril Connolly while married
(1948–50) to Mark Culme-Seymour's half-sister (and Connolly's friend) Janetta
Slater (b. 1922), née Woolley.

[2] Gas attacks, used on the Western Front from 1915, marked the start of
the Battle of the Lys (the fourth battle of Ypres), 9–29 April 1918, part of a
final attempt by the German army to break through Allied lines before the
arrival of American troops. But Bowra is surely also referring to Cyril
Connolly's breaking free from his relationship with his mistress, Lys Lubbock,
to embark on his second marriage, to Barbara Skelton, in October 1950.

[3] In 1951 Sylvester (6/1) and Pauline Gates lived at 5 Cheyne Walk, in
Chelsea.

[4] Robert Newton (1905–56), four-times-married brother of Pauline Gates
and Joy Newton (see next note); actor whose most famous role was Long
John Silver in the 1950 Walt Disney film of *Treasure Island*. His career was
damaged by the alcoholism which eventually killed him.

[5] Joy Newton (1908–74), daughter of the painter Algernon Newton and
sister of Pauline Gates; she married her fourth husband, Den Craig, in 1947.

Straight he shoots and strikes the Mark,[1]
Breaks into the Den,[2]
Gnashes bodies like a shark,
Hurls them to the slimy dark,
Tears the love-nest down – and then
All is still again.

28 April 1951

---

[1] Mark Culme-Seymour.
[2] Dennis ('Den') Craig (1906–72), son of 1st Viscount Craigavon, the first Prime Minister of Northern Ireland; Magdalen 1924–5; author of books on horse-racing. His first wife Aline was the girl who had captivated Bowra in Ireland (see p. xxix above); Joy Newton was his second wife.

John Edward

John Edward[1] was a Norwood boy,
A frolicsome and forward boy,
In work and games was all his joy
On windy Marlborough lea.
He swam through rivers like a trout,
He knew what history's about,
His gamesome cock went shooting out
At all he chanced to see.

John Edward's in his study, and there's spunk upon the floor;
The little fags run in and out, and still he asks for more.
He's a Brackenbury Scholar who's left childish things behind
And knows what future's waiting for a first-class mind –
But he looks into the looking-glass and dark suspicions creep
That daily he grows liker to an old half-witted sheep.

John Edward's up at Balliol and moves among the great,
He drinks his burgundy at noon and dines alone in state –

---

§ The first section of this poem appears to echo 'The story of Augustus
who would not have any soup' in *Der Struwwelpeter* (40/5), despite the
metrical differences; the second section is a parody of 'Drake's Drum' by
Henry Newbolt, in *Admirals All*, 1897.

[1] John Edward Bowle (1905–85), historian; educated at Marlborough College
during the headmastership of Cyril Norwood (1875–1956); Balliol history 1924–7
(Brackenbury Scholar but only achieved a Third); Senior History Master at
Westminster School 1932–40; Lecturer in Modern History, Wadham, 1947–9;
Director, Preparatory Session, College of Europe, Bruges, 1949; Professor of
Political Theory, Bruges, 1950–67. Bowra apparently dubbed him 'that inverted
Bowle we call the sky', *Young Betjeman* (xxv/2), 169; the catastrophic effect of
drink on his academic achievements and career prospects (though hardly as
great as Bowra suggests) passed into Oxford legend. Although an inspirational
teacher, Bowle was 'interminably long-winded and took himself very seriously',
according to Candida Lycett Green – *Letters*, vol. 2 (xxvi/4), 409 – and his
sense of grievance and constant assertion of his own first-class intellectual
abilities became notorious amongst his acquaintance.

But he looks on Ketton-Cremer[1] and sees the chances pass,
And his love is sick within him, and he vomits on the grass,
While Connolly is lurking near to speak a poisoned word
And Sligger[2] grieves that very soon he'll get a double Third.

John Edward is at Westminster, and many are his joys
In expounding Harold Laski[3] to the better-looking boys,
While Betjeman and Bosie[4] gape to watch his soaring star
And London intellectuals come round from near and far –
But David's taken to the girls and Bryan's grown too big,[5]
And nothing's left for him to do but totter home and frig.

John Edward's gone to Oxford assured of high renown,
His head bowed down with learning he saunters up and down.
He's up to All Souls level now, and his dining rights are sweet
And every vacant fellowship is up his special street –
But Christie's[6] come to Jesus and passed the rumour round
That his sexual behaviour is very far from sound.

---

[1] Wyndham Ketton-Cremer (1906–69), author; a Balliol contemporary of Bowle, as was Cyril Connolly (1903–74), author, editor and critic.

[2] Francis Urquhart (1868–1934), Fellow and Tutor (from 1916 Dean) of Balliol 1896–1934; Evelyn Waugh used to sing 'The Dean of Balliol sleeps with men' to the tune of 'Here we go gathering nuts in May' under Urquhart's window.

[3] Laski (1893–1950) expounded socialism (with a Marxist flavour during the 1930s) while Professor of Political Science, London School of Economics and Political Science, 1926–50.

[4] Lord Alfred Douglas (1870–1945), poet, editor, friend of Oscar Wilde. Brian Urquhart (see next note) recounts an occasion when Bosie was Bowle's guest at Westminster's annual Latin Play, a grand public occasion which as usual starred the prettiest King's Scholar, suitably costumed and made up, as the heroine: 'there was, at the first entrance of the heroine, an admiring silence and a sort of corporate intake of breath, which was broken when a voice was heard to say, in fluting Edwardian tones, "Gad, that's an attwactive boy." [. . .] Lord Alfred was hustled out.' *A Life in Peace and War*, 1987, 23.

[5] These are probably references to two of Bowle's pupils at Westminster: David Huxley (1915–92), who became an eminent lawyer in Bermuda, then an investment adviser in New York; and Brian Urquhart (b. 1919), who went on to hold many senior posts in the United Nations, including that of Under-Secretary-General 1974–86.

[6] John Christie (1899–1980), Headmaster of Westminster School 1937–49, then Principal of Jesus.

John Edward's gone to Europe, and a college owns his sway;
To postgraduate researchers he lectures night and day.
He's waiting for his wardenship, and then he'll take his throne
With the finest reputations and come into his own –
But a Belgian crook has tricked him and drummed him out of
   town
With nothing of his glory but a tattered cap and gown.

John Edward shambles down the street to beg a crumb of bread,
His mother trails behind him and shakes a doleful head;
His friends have stabbed him in the back, his boys have run
   away,
And Chandler Bowle[1] refuses to have him home to stay.
So sorrowful a spectacle was surely never seen –
But he was Sligger's pupil, and he was Balliol's queen,
And though new generations come, they'll never never find
Such a Brackenbury Scholar, such a first-class mind.

9 May 1951

---

[1] John Edward's father, a corn merchant in Salisbury, detested by his son
'almost to the point of parricide': *Young Betjeman* (xxv/2), 280.

Election Songs

I

Fools, why make this silly fuss?
I'm your only genius.[1]
I will fit you up with jobs,
Introduce you to the nobs.
Uncle Leslie loves you all;
Listen wisely to his call.
Make your minds up. Better treat me
Nicely; for you can't defeat me.

Lawyer, Papist, Philistine,
Vote upon the good Rowse line.
Warden Sumner's dying soul
Told me I must take control.
Cosy queens and sexy stoats,
Come and cast for me your votes.
I will purify the College
From the curse of useless knowledge.

---

§ The death in April 1951 of Humphrey Sumner (1893–1951), Warden of All
Souls, led to a hotly contested election to choose his successor. Among the
main contenders were Sir Eric Beckett (1896–1966), the candidate proposed by
A. L. Rowse (who, *pace* Bowra, was not himself a candidate), John Sparrow
and Isaiah Berlin. The contest developed into a battle between the supporters
of Beckett and those implacably opposed to any suggestion of direct or
indirect rule by Rowse. Hubert Henderson, who was eventually elected
Warden but is not mentioned in this poem, was a last-minute compromise
candidate chosen to resolve the stalemate. His health broke down almost at
once; after his resignation in January 1952, and a further election campaign,
Sparrow defeated Rowse to become Warden. The subjects of the three songs
(and their singers in the first two cases) are Rowse, Sparrow and Berlin; the
literary models on which the songs are based are the 'Dies Irae', Macaulay's
Lays of Ancient Rome, 1842, and the sea-shanty 'Blow the man down'.

[1] A. L(eslie) Rowse (1903–97), historian specialising in Elizabethan England,
was notorious for his egocentricity and his inflated opinion of his own merits.

[123]

Make me Warden, and I'll rule
You like naughty boys at school.
I will put Isaiah down,
Drive Goronwy out of town,
Out with Cooper, out with Carr[1] –
That's the way with ALR.
If John[2] tries to be too clever,
I will shut his mouth for ever.

Brightly will the College flame
In the glory of my name,
Dizzy with a wild success
Guided by its good Queen Bess.
Who is left to grump or growse
When you're all in love with Rowse?
Vote upon the party-ticket.
Here's my bottom. Come and lick it.

II

Come, Holloway[3] and Holladay,[4]
    Lay bare your hearts to me.
I want to make you break away
    From all you'd like to be.
Let flow the salt, sweet tears, and lay
    Your heads upon my knee.

A College is no roadhouse bar
    To treat the passing trull,
Nor rowdy nightclub kept by Carr
    To keep his pockets full,

---

[1] Goronwy Rees (84/4), John Cooper (1920–78) and Raymond Carr (154/1) had been leaders of the Berlin campaign.

[2] John Sparrow (14/2), determined defender of the All Souls status quo, was Warden of All Souls 1952–77.

[3] John Holloway (1920–99), Fellow of All Souls 1946–60, distinguished poet.

[4] James Holladay (1921–89), Fellow of All Souls 1947–49.

Where randy runts for partners spar
    And Monteith[1] plays the bull.

Here is no place for women's bowers
    And softly scented mists;
Dons should ascend the Hawksmoor towers[2]
    To keep their amorous trysts;
Or concentrate their sexual powers
    On well-bred Wykehamists.

Fling open Codrington's great door,
    Let Craster[3] cease to crow.
Victorian sermons, hide no more
    But unction sweet bestow,
And misplaced commas by the score
    Delight the biblio.

Where Chapel walls have empty space
    Let artists show their skill.
Let Ward and Etty scatter grace
    And Landseer give a thrill,
And in the Common Room I'll place
    An early Pickersgill.[4]

---

[1] Charles Monteith (1921–95), publisher, Fellow of All Souls 1948–88.

[2] The architect Nicholas Hawksmoor (1661–1736) designed a major extension of All Souls: his new northern quadrangle is dominated by two towers to the east, flanking the common-room, and by the Codrington Library to the north.

[3] Edmund Craster (1879–1959), Fellow and at the time Librarian of All Souls.

[4] James Ward (1769–1859), William Etty (1787–1849), Edwin Landseer (1802–73) and Henry Pickersgill (1782–1875), British painters whose work Sparrow, a keen art-collector, particularly favoured.

No need for College Meetings now
   The cry for change has gone.
Bert[1] will instruct the Fellows how
   The business should be done,
And no research will I allow
   But on Mark Pattison.[2]

III [3]

In aprons and oilskins and torn dungarees,
With wild eyes aflame and hair spread on the breeze,
From the bin and the brothel, the tiles and the tote,
We've marched up to Oxford to hand in our vote;
You may want an impeccable yes-man from town,
But we'll huff and we'll puff and we'll blow the man
   down.[4]

To Hell with tradition. We do as we wish
And think that roast mallard's[5] a damned rotten dish;
A nice cafeteria open to all
Means much more to us than a dinner in Hall.
Sing hey diddle, there's blood on the foam.
Isaiah's our man, and we'll see he gets home.

---

[1] Bert(ram) Watson (1914–89), Manciple of All Souls.

[2] Mark Pattison (1813–84), Rector of Lincoln College. For many years Sparrow hoped to write a biography of Pattison, but the nearest he got was *Mark Pattison and the Idea of a University*, 1967 (the 1965 Clark lectures), and an edition of Pattison's *Memoirs* which, though it reached page-proof, remained unpublished, because of a handful of ludicrously pedantic disagreements between Sparrow and his publisher, Colin Haycraft of Duckworth. The proofs are in the Codrington Library, together with relevant correspondence. Will someone come to the rescue?

[3] The rallying cry of the rebellious younger element at All Souls (sometimes known as the 'sans-culottes'), supporters of Isaiah Berlin.

[4] Cf. 'I'll huff and I'll puff and I'll blow your house down!' in the children's story, *The Three Little Pigs*.

[5] The mallard is the emblem of All Souls; roast duck is the traditional fare at the annual All Souls Gaudy.

We put up with no nonsense in College affairs,
We stand for free fucking behind the back stairs.
We'll take on the Chapel and make it a stew
And punt all the trust funds on any old screw.
So *brekekekex* and *koax* and *koax*;[1]
We'll do all that we can for the beast with two backs.

Though the old rat Dunbabin[2] gnaws under the floor,
We'll bash him and smash him and thrash him galore;
If the stuffed sausage Jacob[3] forgets his right place
We'll snub him and drub him and fart in his face.
Then hey tally-ho, tooraloo for Big B,
Sing the red dean, the dead dean, dean Sparrow and we.[4]

Though Falls[5] may talk big of a counter-attack
We'll make him skedaddle with crabs on his back;
Though Craster may threaten us all with the dock,
We'll send him to bed with a louse on his cock.
Tarara-tarara and boom-boom-de-ay,[6]
We'll talk till our speeches have darkened the day.

---

[1] From the onomatopoeic refrain of the chorus of frogs in Aristophanes' eponymous comedy.

[2] Thomas Dunbabin (1911–55), archaeologist, Fellow and Domestic Bursar of All Souls at the time of the election.

[3] Ernest Jacob (1894-1971), Chichele Professor of Modern History from 1950; Fellow of All Souls, and a candidate himself during the early stages of the election plotting.

[4] These rather baffling references ought from the context to be to Berlin's supporters. But Sparrow was a rival, as (in Bowra's version) was Rowse, the recently retired Junior Dean of All Souls and hence arguably the 'dead dean'. Perhaps the line refers, somewhat bewilderingly, to all three candidates, making the 'red dean' Berlin himself, by analogy with another notorious thorn in the Establishment's side, Hewlett Johnson, the 'Red Dean' of Canterbury Cathedral. Other interpretations are undoubtedly possible.

[5] Cyril Falls (1888–1971), military correspondent of *The Times* 1939–53, Chichele Professor of the History of War and Fellow of All Souls 1946–53; one of Rowse's most committed supporters.

[6] 'Ta-ra-ra-boom-de-ay' is the title and refrain of a song by Richard Morton popularised by the music-hall star Lottie Collins in 1891.

We'll laugh in the face of the gaunt guillotine
Which Rowse says he'll use if we say what we mean.
We shall knit as we sit and watch him go by
With defeat in his heart and despair in his eye.
So hey zing-a-zing and bom-a-bom-boom[1] –
When Rowse dies of fury we'll dance on his tomb.

16 June 1951

---

[1] Cf. 'Zing-a zing-a boom boom' from the 1950 Dean Martin song 'Zing-a zing-a zing boom'.

Sabbatum Regium

Bingo, Bingo, stir the stew;
Crackerjack and Bugaboo,
Fling in punk and copper's nark,
Namier[1] and clammy Clark,[2]
Oozy gobs of Webster[3] with
Dollops of dissolving Smith,[4]
Dribble softly in the pan
Yellow drip of Masterman.[5]

§ Doubtless inspired by the Three Witches in *Macbeth*, 'Sabbatum Regium' ('Kings' Sabbath') sets the scene for the 1957 election of the Regius Professor of Modern History, Oxford, caused by the impending retirement of V. H. Galbraith. Although nominally a Crown appointment, the Regius Professor is in practice chosen by the Prime Minister, acting on advice from within the University and from eminent historians outside it. In early 1957 Anthony Eden, the then Prime Minister, and the current Vice-Chancellor of Oxford, A. H. Smith, were believed to favour A. J. P. Taylor (130/2) to succeed Galbraith. But both men retired on health grounds and the incoming Prime Minister, Harold Macmillan (75/§), and Vice-Chancellor, J. C. Masterman, had different views. Bowra assumes (with some imaginative licence) that the four leading candidates were Taylor, Hugh Trevor-Roper, R. W. Southern and A. L. Rowse (123/1), and devotes a stanza each to their characterisation.

[1] Sir Lewis Namier (1888–1960), Professor of Modern History, Manchester, 1931–53; born in Polish Galicia (hence presumably 'the Pole' referred to in the third stanza); a friend and adviser of Harold Macmillan, who consulted him about the candidates.

[2] G(eorge) N. Clark (1890–1979), Regius Professor of Modern History, Cambridge, 1943–47; Provost of Oriel 1947–57. (The Regius Professor is a Fellow of Oriel.)

[3] Charles Webster (1886–1961), Professor of International History, London School of Economics and Political Science, 1932–53.

[4] Alic Smith (1883–1958), philosopher; Warden of New College, 1944–58; Vice-Chancellor, Oxford, 1954–7; the strain of the Vice-Chancellorship fatally undermined his health.

[5] John Masterman (1891–1977), historian, Student of Christ Church 1919–46 (where he had been Trevor-Roper's tutor); Provost of Worcester 1946–61; Vice-Chancellor, Oxford, 1957–8.

Brew and chew and let your breath
Waft the reek of dead Galbraith.[1]

Weeping, creeping crocodiles,
Gnarled and snarled with pox and piles,
Shooting glassy grins about,
Swivelling a snooty snout,
When the Taylor[2] flaps his tail,
Crack your jaws and snap out 'Hail!'

Eyes of cod in spawning shoal,
Bleared with blinking round the Pole,
Body smooth as baby's bum,
Twice to bed and nothing come,
Blake[3] and rake[4] and God knows who
Heat and eat the shit for Hugh.[5]

---

[1] V(ivian) H. Galbraith (1889–1976), Regius Professor of Modern History,
Oxford, 1947–57, the outgoing occupant of the Chair – hence dead in a
professional sense.

[2] A(lan) J. P. Taylor (1906–90), historian and journalist; Lecturer in
Modern History, Manchester, 1930–8 (from 1931 under Namier); Fellow (and
Tutor in Modern History until 1963) of Magdalen 1938–76; Lecturer in
International History, Oxford, 1953–63. A committed and outspoken socialist,
he nevertheless enjoyed good living (hence perhaps the accusation of
hypocrisy?); and although his major work on the causes of the Second World
War lay ahead, he had already concluded that Hitler was an opportunist rather
than a leader uniquely evil in his intentions, a view frequently misinterpreted
as an exoneration of Hitler. The front-runner in the election's early stages,
Taylor blamed Masterman and his own mentor, Namier, for his eventual
failure to be elected.

[3] Robert Blake (1916–2003), Baron Blake 1971; historian, Student and Tutor
in Politics, Christ Church 1947–68; Provost of Queen's 1968–87; a leading
supporter of Trevor-Roper's candidacy for the Regius Professorship.

[4] Perhaps Ray(mond) C(arr) (154/1).

[5] The candidate eventually appointed, Hugh Trevor-Roper (1914–2003; Lord
Dacre of Glanton 1979; Student of Christ Church 1946–57; Regius Professor of
Modern History and Fellow of Oriel 1957–80; Master of Peterhouse,
Cambridge, 1980–7); anti-clerical and iconoclastic but nevertheless more
conservative in his views than Taylor and hence more acceptable to many of
those concerned. He wore thick pebble spectacles and was for much of his life
of misleadingly youthful appearance; his marriage to Lady Alexandra Howard-
Johnston, who had three children from an earlier marriage, was childless (and
the subject of some speculation).

Where the Pickwick capers[1] call,
Where the papal shadows fall,
Where the dead nuns stir and stare,
Fog and fever everywhere,
Ghouls and Gallowglasses,[2] rise
Sodden under Southern[3] skies.

Brows on which the thunder rolls,
Eyes as black as fallen souls,
In the potencies of sex
Artifex and opifex,[4]
God to whom the world's a louse,
Who can crack its back but Rowse?[5]

Bingo, stir the pot and then
Count the score to number ten,[6]
One and one, and two and two,
Let the vampires sniff the stew,

---

[1] Possibly a play on words inspired by F. M. Powicke (1879–1963), medieval historian and Regius Professor 1928–47, who after his retirement was based in Southern's college, Balliol, and would be assumed to support him in the election campaign.

[2] Irish mercenaries of Scottish descent, mentioned in *Macbeth*. Here possibly a reference to the line of medieval historians with northern links and connections to Balliol – Thomas Tout (1855–1929; Professor of History, Manchester, 1890–1925), Powicke and Galbraith – a line continued by Southern.

[3] Richard Southern (1912–2001), Fellow of Balliol 1937–61; Chichele Professor of Modern History, Oxford, 1961–9; a medieval historian, born in Newcastle. He made his name with *The Making of the Middle Ages* (1953), written while he was recovering from tuberculosis; major sections of this work deal with the papacy and the monasteries.

[4] The creative artist and the worker – from a mnemonic jingle about Latin gender: 'Common are to either sex / Artifex and opïfex [. . .]'. John Barrow Allen, *An Elementary Latin Grammar*, 2nd ed., 1877, 118, §154 (*b*).

[5] A. L. Rowse (123/1), renowned for his high opinion of himself and contempt for almost everyone else; a homosexual, he prided himself on combining scholarly research with the writing of poetry.

[6] 10 Downing Street.

Let them preen and prang and prance
Up and down in ding-dong dance,
Stepping in and stepping out,
Bull and bully, twirp and tout,[1]
Let them suck the sickly sud
Of each other's brains and blood,
Till the stroke of midnight falls,
And they flop like eunuch's balls.

10 March 1957

---

[1] Presumably the four candidates, but in which order? And does 'tout' refer to the historian of that name (131/2)? Readers are invited to judge for themselves.

Momotombo

Momotombo, the pedigree pom,
Tombo-tombo-tombo-tom,
Flutters, and flirts, and beams, and beguiles
Gelded youth with his smirks and smiles;
Crowned with a splendour of silk-soft hair,
Sugared and stuffed like a brown éclair,
Like a warm, wet sewer he ripples and purls,
Queen Boase in the Boase-bed garden of girls.[1]

No Jews got the jute[2] where he comes from;
Tombo-tombo-tombo-tom,
On waves of chitterchat whisked and whirled,
He purrs and chirrs through the huge high world.
Wider and wider his bounds are set,
Till he knows those best whom he has not met.
He wrings out a secret from everyone
And serves it up fresh as a hot-cross bun.

---

§ Momotombo is the name of a volcano in Nicaragua; stylistically this
poem echoes T. S. Eliot's *Old Possum's Book of Practical Cats.* Thomas ('Tom')
Boase (1898–1974), historian and art administrator, amateurish and largely
ineffectual Director of the Courtauld Institute of Art and Professor of History
of Art, London, 1937–47; President of Magdalen 1947–68; Vice-Chancellor of
Oxford 1958–60 (Bowra's successor but two); like Bowra he gathered round
him a 'salon' of young admirers. Alan Pryce-Jones recalled Bowra's reaction to
the election of the 'slightly spinsterish' Boase as President of Magdalen:
'Extraordinary thing that the Fellows of Magdalen should choose as their
President a man of no public virtues and no private parts.' Alan Pryce-Jones,
The Bonus of Laughter, 1987, 229.

[1] In 1952–3 Boase led a campaign to install a rose-garden commemorating
the inventors of penicillin (paid for by an American donor, Mrs Mary Lasker,
and designed by Sylvia Crowe) on Magdalen land next to Oxford's Botanic
Garden; the opposition, orchestrated by John Betjeman, argued that the
proposal was too suburban for Oxford's High Street. Boase proved the astuter
campaigner, and the rose-garden was created. Subsequent references to Boase
by Bowra and Betjeman often include rose-related word-plays. For details see
Bevis Hillier, 'The Boase Garden', *Betjemanian,* vol. 9, 1997–8, 10–38.

[2] Boase's birth-place, Dundee, was known for its jute industry.

His eyes are upturned to the starry dome,
Tombo-tombo-tombo-tom,
His topsail is trimmed to all winds that blow
Low to the high and high to the low;
To him the envious Graces[1] yield
The juiciest fruits of the Potter's Field,[2]
And carpet his path on the windy lea
With blossoms blown from the Judas-tree.

He flips and flaps in the Muses' home,
Tombo-tombo-tombo-tom,
Pen and pencil and chisel and brush
Kindle the flames of his burning bush.
The faintest approaches of Beauty start
A gush and a gulp in his jellied heart,
And red is the light that glows on his cheek
When she gives his bottom a teasing tweak.

He is the playgirls' and playboys' mom,
Tombo-tombo-tombo-tom,
They sigh to be swathed in his swaddling form
And thirst for the burst of his brimming storm.
Oozily, oozily, drip, drip, drip,
He promises prowess in bedmanship,
But where is the solace for breaking hearts,
When there's nothing but wind in his private parts?

18 March 1957

---

[1] The three Graces, Aglaia (splendour), Euphrosyne (festivity) and Thalia (rejoicing), were alleged to bring peace and happiness.
[2] The Pharisees bought a potter's field with the 30 pieces of silver returned to them by Judas before he hanged himself; it was used as a cemetery for foreigners and hence became known as the Field of Blood.

Lord Boothby Enters Heaven

Hallelujah and hullaballoo,
Baron de Boothby[1] ascends through the blue.
Haloes encircle his snow-soft hair,
Shattering, scattering stars in the air.
Cherubim leap from the groaning board,
Hurtle to welcome the risen lord;
Thrones and Dominions and Powers rejoice,
Rapt in the spell of that golden voice,
Dulcet as dew-drops and deep as the sea,
Heard on a Sunday from ITV.[2]
All the Elect with a loud 'Hear, hear!'
Burst in applause for the peerless peer.
Balmy, benevolent, winsome and wise,
Father-figure to all in the skies,
Blandly he strides to the tip-top place,
Ready to sit on the Throne of Grace.
Old cock Jehovah must off and away;
Boothby is here and has come to stay.
In black immensities down below
Mumbles of misery, wails of woe,

§ A parody of Vachel Lindsay's poetic tribute to the founder of the
Salvation Army, 'General William Booth Enters into Heaven' (*General William
Booth Enters into Heaven and Other Poems*, 1919), which was set to the tune of
'Are You Washed in the Blood of the Lamb?' by Charles Ives.

[1] Robert Boothby (75/§) had been created Baron Boothby of Buchan and
Rattray Head earlier in 1958.

[2] BBC TV's *In the News* (1950–5), offering discussion between iconoclasts,
was a great success, and its four regular panellists (Boothby, A. J. P. Taylor
[130/2], Michael Foot and the Independent MP W. J. Brown) became known
as the Famous Four. The programme, shown at Sunday lunchtime, transferred
to ITV on the the latter's inception in 1955 (still featuring the Famous Four),
was renamed *Free Speech*, and continued until 1961.

Potentates stretched on the raw, red rack,
Blubbering vainly for whiskered Mac.[1]
Down the Conservative ladies crash
Under the shriek of the serpent-lash;
Turds, as he sinks in a squelching bog,
Stuff up the pores and the paunch of Hogg;[2]
Greasy and queasy from dank, dark drains
Rats scrabble over the Salisbury[3] plains;
Red-hot pokers up Pickthorn's[4] arse
Sizzle and frizzle his guts of brass.
Little the Lord on his golden chair
Recks what befalls to the fallen there.

What is this multitude pale as pearls,
Preening and queening like teenage girls?
Twittering, flittering, squawks and screams,
Swooping in droves on its land of dreams?
Pansies and buttercups out on a beano
In the celestial Kleist Casino?[5]
Wobble of buttocks and flutter of hair,
Kisses and hisses adrift on the air,
Shampooed goats from a scapegoat flock
Curtsy in awe to the master's cock,
Hail the Deliverer, massive and male –
Can such virility faint or fail? –
Blossom and burst in the sunshine glow,
Scattering seed on the world below.

---

[1] Harold Macmillan (75/§).

[2] Rt Hon Quintin Hogg (1907–2001), 2nd Viscount Hailsham 1950–63, Baron Hailsham of St Marylebone 1970; barrister, QC and Conservative politician, at the time of this poem Lord President of the Council and chairman of the Conservative Party.

[3] Robert ('Bobbety') Gascoyne-Cecil (1893–1972), 5th Marquess of Salisbury, Conservative politician who had resigned from the Cabinet in 1957.

[4] Kenneth Pickthorn (1892–1975), constitutional historian and Conservative MP.

[5] A 'queer' night club in Berlin.

Out of the sunset a fragrant throng
Leaps with a bustle of dance and song.
Ladies as lovely as youth's desire
Burnish their limbs in a pubic fire.
Airily, fairily deep dark eyes
Gleam through the dusk of the summer skies.
Rumble and tumble of lips and limbs,
Eager advances from thirsty quims,
Wibble and wobble of sex on show
Set every bottom and breast aglow.
Sprightly sopranos in concord raise
Songs to the master and sound his praise.
Into his nostrils the incense whirls.
Bob's in his Heaven. All's right with the girls.[1]

7 December 1958

---

[1] Cf. 'God's in His heaven – / All's right with the world.' Robert Browning, song from the play *Pippa Passes*, 1841.

The Dead Dean

Sunk beneath the spotted laurels,
Where the bleak begonias blow,
Deaf to canons' quirks and quarrels,
Back to start as Prairie Joe,
　　Lies Dean Lowe.

Oh delirious trance of twirling
Gaitered calves and buckled shoon,
In the waltz or one-step whirling
Till co-eds of Saskatoon
　　Swished aswoon.

Fizz in plated tankards foaming,
Bellyfuls of Britain's best,
Port and brandy in the gloaming;
Beer and cider must contest
　　For the rest.

As a stallion streaks from stable
Frenzy-frothed in rutting pain,
Charged he to the green-baize table,
Whereon bluff and bounce attain
　　Game and gain.

---

§ The subject is the Very Revd John Lowe (1899–1960), Dean of Christ
Church (where he had earlier been a Rhodes Scholar) 1939–59, Vice-Chancellor
of Oxford 1948–51 (Bowra's immediate predecessor in that office, who had
taken precedence over Bowra in 1948 only because Bowra was on a working
visit to Harvard when the previous Vice-Chancellor died suddenly). Lowe was
born and spent most of his life in Canada – his obituary refers to 'his
inevitably limited knowledge of the English scene in general' (*The Times*, 12
August 1960, 13); his specialism was the New Testament, on which he often
preached. Although his final episode of illness started in late 1957, his death
did not occur until more than eighteen months after the apparent date of this
poem: is the date a later mistake, had Bowra received premature news of
Lowe's demise, or does the poem represent wishful thinking?

Collect, Gospel and Epistle,
Grace by copes and albs renewed –
How the dental plates would whistle,
Cheeks and chaps and chin exude
    Faith and food.

Stunned infinitives went sprawling,
Split in twain from top to toe;
Uplift waves of discourse falling
Spumed in Transatlantic flow
    Harsh and slow.

Meaty lips, the Bible twanging,
Spread a guilty, goose-flesh gloom;
Like a brazen cymbal clanging,
Word on word would blare and boom
    Strokes of doom.

God's green world was his for soaking,
Plants and plots the livelong way . . .
In his mouth the worms come poking;
It has nothing now to say
    To the clay.

Roots and tubers crack the sockets
Where the blood ran rude and red;
Slug and maggot pick the pockets
Where the cash was put to bed.
    Dean Lowe's dead.

15 December 1958

Prize song

Green with lust and sick with shyness,
Let me lick your lacquered toes.
Gosh, oh gosh, your Royal Highness,
Put your finger up my nose,
Pin my teeth upon your dress,
Plant my head with watercress.

Only you can make me happy.
Tuck me tight beneath your arm.
Wrap me in a woollen nappy;
Let me wet it till it's warm.
In a plush and plated pram
Wheel me round St James's, Ma'am.

Let your sleek and soft galoshes
Slide and slither on my skin.
Swaddle me in mackintoshes
Till I lose my sense of sin.
Lightly plant your plimsolled heel
Where my privy parts congeal.

---

§ The speaker is John Betjeman (15/§), who on 18 December 1958 received
the annual Duff Cooper Prize – a cheque for £150 and a copy of Duff
Cooper's memoirs bound in leather – from his friend Her Royal Highness
Princess Margaret (1930–2002). The judges had been Lord David Cecil, Harold
Nicolson and (as chairman) Bowra himself. Duff Cooper's widow Diana
observed that 'Poor Betch was crying and too moved to find an apology for
words' (Philip Ziegler, *Diana Cooper*, 1981, 310). Stylistically the poem mimics
Betjeman's own 'In Westminster Abbey', in *Old Lights for New Chancels*
(xxvi/3).

Clothe yourself in dark-blue bloomers;
Swing me round on your trapeze.
In your bosom, like a puma's,
Let me stroke your stockinged knees.
Batter me with Indian clubs
While I nuzzle in your bubs.

Tea and biscuits at the Palace,
Till the Holy Spirit hails,
And we taste the selfsame chalice,
Share a wafer at the rails,
Breathe the Gospel's breezy balm,
Sweetly sweating palm in palm.

Hell may vomit flames to seize us;
On our scooters we'll away,
With no company but Jesus
Through the smog of Judgement Day,
Till God's Gothic gasolier
Tips the wink that all is clear.

Calvin, Irving, Spurgeon,[1] guide me
To the Salem of the Saints.
Tip-top-lady,[2] mount astride me
Till my risen body faints
And in gobs of glowing goo
Bursts and burbles under you.

1 January 1959

---

[1] John Calvin (1509–64), French religious reformer and preacher, exponent
of the doctrine of predestination; a bête noire of Bowra's (see p. xxi). Edward
Irving (1792–1834), Scottish preacher who came to London and inspired the
foundation of the Catholic Apostolic Church. Charles Haddon Spurgeon
(1834–92), Baptist preacher.
[2] A reference to the Revd Augustus Toplady (1740–78), who wrote the
words of the hymn which begins: 'Rock of ages, cleft for me, / Let me hide
myself in thee'.

Babes in the Wood

Airs and Graces float to greet them
Pearly from the Atlantic spray;
Trolls and trollops cannot cheat them
On the windy-wendy way,
By coquetting breezes fanned
To the Never-Never-Land.

With a roof of sugar-candy,
Golden walls of gingerbread,
Always ready, always randy,
With a bear-skin for a bed,
Till their grunts and giggles roll
To the pole-star from the pole.

Sundew and narcissus hold them
In the soft synthetic spring;
Dawn and dusk have rocked and rolled them
Till their haunches laugh and sing,
All the ghoulish gossip past,
They are safe at home at last.

High the fanes of Princeton tower
Through the blank electric blaze;
Higher is the tree-top bower,
Where the dewy love-nest sways,
Cradled in the bluebell sky,
Where no prigs can poke or pry.

---

§ The affair between Renée Ayer (34/1) and Stuart Hampshire (59/1),
philosopher, began in the mid 1930s, but they did not marry until 1961.
Hampshire's role as co-respondent in the Ayer divorce in 1942 damaged his
academic career, particularly at Oxford; he was Grote Professor of Philosophy
of Mind and Logic, London, 1960–63 and Professor of Philosophy, Princeton,
1963–70, returning to succeed Bowra as Warden of Wadham.

All the wounds so foully dealt them
Heal in one long, locked embrace.
Love and logic merge to melt them
As they slither base to base.
Dance again the blotted years
To the heart-strings of the spheres.

Ah, but agues creak and crackle
On the blind besotted lawn,
Jackals and hyenas cackle,
Alligators spume and spawn.
Where the blistered night begins,
Footless frogs wind widdershins.

Crabs and flukes and lice come creeping
Dankly down the slobbered track;
Buttock upon buttock leaping,
Rats and skunks ride pick-a-back;
Pink amoebas spot the floor,
Termites yawn and ask for more.

Planets reel through belching thunder,
Lightnings strip the twittering trees,
Hurricanes rip moons asunder,
Bodies melt in grimy grease.
Queasy spires of Fairy Town
Cringe and crack and hurtle down.

Sneering Doom has tracked and found them,
Trapped the happy, helpless pair.
Demons prance grimacing round them,
As they shiver blue and bare,
Searching the sarcastic skies,
Weeping for the dream that dies.

22 May 1963

The Deserted Warden

The deadlong night, the livelong day
    I waste and weep alone.
Dank wizened leaves of pride and play
    Upon my heart are strewn.
In rooms where laughs rang gross and gay
    Are gloom and grief and groan.

Outside my window swells a tower
    Whose parts assault the skies.
Where flushed and blushed a rosy bower
    Shapeless abortions rise,
And organs of unpitying power
    Breathe murder in my eyes.

No Gothick graces shed their spell
    On finial or groin.
No gargoyles and no dripstops tell
    Their tale to cusp or coign,

---

§ In the early months of 1965 the Commission of Inquiry into Oxford
University, chaired by Lord Franks, turned its attention towards All Souls,
within which a battle was already raging about the future direction of the
College, its responsibilities towards the other, less well-off, University
institutions and the best use for its surplus funds. One option was an increase
in the number of Research Fellows and the erection of a building to house
them within the college, on the east side of the Warden's garden. Although
architects' plans were drawn up, the scheme was eventually abandoned
(147/§), *pace* the imagined outcome in the poem. The radical element in All
Souls blamed the notoriously conservative Warden John Sparrow, the speaker
in this poem, for delaying tactics designed to stifle this and other proposals
for change.

The poem is dated the day following the Franks Commission's examination
of All Souls, but the despairing tone surely reflects Sparrow's earlier mood, as
the Commission's treatment of All Souls on that occasion was relatively gentle.
The story continues in the next poem; both poems are in the poetic format of
Lewis Carroll's nonsense poem 'The Mad Gardener's Song' from *Sylvie and
Bruno*, 1889, but it is not clear whether the echo is intentional.

But faceless slabstones, foul and fell,
    Their rasping discords join.

I wished to take their ill-got wealth
    And hand it to the poor,
But They purloined it all by stealth
    And spent it aft and fore.
They've cracked my mind, they've crocked my health,
    And still they ask for more.

The jaunty jade of Richmond Hill[1]
    Twirls her plump buttocks round;
The Fisher King[2] stands to the kill;
    Hogs[3] belch and burst and bound,
And coats[4] of many hues distil
    Black blood-clots on the ground.

The Stuart[5] tartan frisks no more,
    The Lion[6] breed is gone.
The manciple has slammed the door
    On those whose day is done;
Far off the hill-top prophet's roar[7]
    Makes globules of the sun.

---

[1] Sir Ian Richmond (1902–65), Professor of the Archaeology of the Roman Empire, Oxford, and Fellow of All Souls 1956–65.

[2] Henry ('Harry') Fisher (1918–2005), barrister, QC and from 1968 High Court judge; Fellow of All Souls 1946–73, Estates Bursar 1961–6, Sub-Warden 1965–7; later President of Wolfson.

[3] Quintin Hogg (136/2), Fellow of All Souls 1931–8 and from 1961.

[4] David Caute (b. 1936; known to friends by his first name, John), novelist and historian, Fellow of All Souls 1959–65; a supporter of a rival scheme for the admission of graduate students to All Souls, he resigned his fellowship when in November 1965 this scheme too was defeated in favour of the election of Visiting Fellows.

[5] Stuart Hampshire (59/1).

[6] Lionel Butler (1923–81), Fellow of All Souls 1946–55, Professor of Medieval History, St Andrews, 1955–73.

[7] Presumably Isaiah Berlin (31/§), Bowra's 'Major Prophet', who lived at the top of Headington Hill after his marriage in 1956.

Their spouts of spit congeal and set
    In walls of frozen spleen;
Shunning the daylight, white and wet
    Each flops, an oozing queen,
And drinking one another's sweat,
    They suckle hate unseen.

So that is why I sit and sit,
    Knowing the end is near.
Dry rot devours me bit by bit,
    My life-springs disappear,
And when I sink into the pit,
    No ghost shall know me here.

12 February 1965

Apotheosis

They planned to plant a topless town[1]
    In the miasmal air,
Whose battlements should growl and frown
    If I set footstep there.
I huffed and puffed and blew them down,
    And who will find them where?

I smote them hip, I smote them thigh,
    Their heads rolled round my feet.
Their bowels puke and putrefy
    With pus for winding-sheet,
And when my nostrils taste them, I
    Find the crude carrion sweet.

---

§ In a letter dated 6 March 1965 to Sylvester Gates, Bowra writes, 'I enclose a poem, a sequel to the last one I sent you. You may perhaps deduce from it that dear John has recovered from his defeats and is on the win. In the meanwhile it is a time to rejoice.' In January 1965 All Souls had instructed its Building Committee to commission revised plans for the proposed new building to house additional Research Fellows (144/§), but Sparrow, an implacable opponent of the new building, took advantage of the commitment to graduate students with which the Franks Commission had been placated to announce in March that the building scheme had been shelved. (The proposed admission of 30 or more graduates would require external accommodation, and so was less objectionable to Sparrow than the planned building within All Souls to house the smaller number of Research Fellows.) Although no formal decision was ever taken by All Souls, Sparrow succeeded in killing the scheme: the poem reflects his jubilation at this impending triumph. For details see David Caute, 'Crisis in All Souls', *Encounter*, March 1966.

Sparrow's single-minded homosexuality was well-known to the circle of friends for whom Bowra wrote. So the total inappropriateness of the heterosexual references reinforces the poem's theme of exultant transformation: for Sparrow to lust after women would have required a metamorphosis as startling as his deification.

[1] Cf. 'the topless towers of Ilium', Christopher Marlowe, *The Tragical History of Dr Faustus*, 1604, scene 13.

From God's great house I peer below
    Into the yawning pit;
Their incandescent bottoms glow
    And sizzle in the shit,
And armoured bedbugs row on row
    Gobble them bit by bit.

I spread my lilac-lacquered wings
    From star to amorous star.
A squad of bum-faced Cherubs sings
    Across the sunset-bar,
And, gleaming at the soul of things,
    I gild my avatar.

Light of the World, Penelope,[1]
    Twist your atomic beam,
Till from the sullied dusk I see
    Veils of Nirvana gleam,
And make my withered tendrils be
    Wet as the wettest dream.

On slices of delicious Pam[2]
    I feed my swelling soul;
My senses reel from flim to flam
    In bawdy barcarolle,
And creamy distillations cram
    My flesh from hole to hole.

---

[1] Penelope Betjeman (21/§, 26/§), with whom Sparrow often went horse-riding, lived in Wantage, near the Atomic Energy Research Establishment at Harwell.

[2] Cf. 'And slices of delicious ham', from 'Jim: The boy who ran away from his nurse and was eaten by a lion', in Hilaire Belloc's *Cautionary Tales for Children*, 1908. Pam is Lady Pamela Berry (1914–1982), society hostess, daughter of 1st Earl of Birkenhead (8/2) and wife of Michael Berry, later Baron Hartwell, proprietor of the *Daily Telegraph*.

Come, Lady Ann,[1] the sails are spread
    To cross the sodden sea.
From Goldeneye[2] to golden bed
    The wind blows fresh and free.
The Gadarene Gagools[3] are fled.
    Come back, come back to me!

Enskied and aureoled I stay
    With moons on every hand.
Mine is the Truth, mine is the Way,
    And on this peak I stand,
Till the bronze blast of Judgement Day
    Shall leave me in command.

6 March 1965

---

[1] Ann Fleming (1913–81), née Charteris, widow of the author Ian Fleming
(who died in 1964); previously married first to 3rd Baron O'Neill, then to 2nd
Viscount Rothermere; a close friend of Bowra (see p. xxx above) and of
Sparrow.

[2] Ian Fleming's house on Jamaica.

[3] Presumably Sparrow's opponents, the would-be modernisers, whose plans
he saw as fatal to the All Souls he wished to preserve. The Gadarene swine of
the Gospels destroyed themselves while possessed by demons; and Gagool, an
evil old witch in H. Rider Haggard's 1885 novel *King Solomon's Mines*, came to
a gruesome end while attempting to lure the heroes to their doom.

APPENDIX

'Hear the weeping crocodiles!'

Hear the weeping crocodiles!
Erika has got the piles.
But the inexorable Dick
Marshals his unfailing prick.
Blood may flow and wind may pass –
He will put it up her arse:
Marching bravely to the front
He will put it up her cunt.
Let the boils burst in her womb,
Let the bride-bed be a tomb –
Keep the flag flying on the pole –
Dick will fill up every hole.
Corpse or carrion matters not:
He will find another twot,
Or if twot be none, why then
He'll be satisfied with men.
Dick has sampled little boys,
Dick has known unnatural joys.

---

§ Bowra did not include this poem, coarse even by his own standards, in
the fair copy of his satires. The object of Bowra's vitriol is Richard Crossman
(1907–74), New College classics 1926–30, Fellow and Tutor in Philosophy
1930–7; Assistant Editor, *New Statesman and Nation*, 1938–55; Labour politician
and eventual Cabinet Minister. In 1932 he embarked on a short-lived marriage
(his first and her third) to German-born Erika Glück. The poem's metrical
form is appropriately reminiscent of Harry Graham's *Ruthless Rhymes for
Heartless Homes*, 1899.

He will take on rougher stuff
If the stud fee be enough.
Service he will give for cheques
On the nail from either sex.
All the nancies, all the he-men
Like the taste of Crossman's semen.
Pelion on Ossa laid
Still insists on being paid.
But what loving friend of Dick's
Knows his catalogue of tricks?
Who has heard the evening hiss
Through the window of his piss?
Who has seen him gaily sit
On his rising smell of shit?
Pondering between his jerks
Pauline views of faith and works?
Ah, he knows to bear the cross,
Take the profits, miss the loss.
Who denies that Crossman can
Show us to be perfect man?

A Weekend in Paris

Returning from two weeks abroad
Jane found her husband far from bored.
He'd fixed to take his lady friend
To Paris for the next weekend.

This did not suit Jane's cup of tea.
In fact she said, 'But what of me?'
'My sweet, I fear you'll be *de trop*
Unless you get another beau.
But time is short, we leave at tea,
And it is now already three.'

My lady, put upon her mettle,
Thought it wise at once to settle
Any more nonsense or largesse
Connected with the Marchioness.
And so she wired with frantic haste
To an admirer of her taste;
Who straight accepted with delight
To help her in her sorry plight.

Now Lady Jane thought it was best
To put her SA to the test,
So vamped her husband all she knew
And murmured loving words and true.
She thought perhaps it would be wise
To cease for once to tantalise.

---

§ The most likely targets of this (possibly incomplete) tale are Kenneth
Clark (13/2) and his wife Jane (13/3). Clark admitted in his autobiographies – *Another Part of the Wood* (xxvii/5) and *The Other Half*, 1977 – that
he was not by nature monogamous, and had often strayed.

And so demure and sweet became
She really hardly seemed the same.

Her husband, up to all her tricks,
Gave back a brace of well-timed kicks,
But as her sweetness did persist,
He found her harder to resist.
And later on towards the end,
He quite forgot his lady friend.
For sure enough she had him taped,
By Monday morning he was raped.

Meanwhile her beau got rather sore.
He thought her escapade a bore,
And neither did he contemplate
Remaining there just as a bait.
So when from Cartier Jane returned,
To flaunt the bracelet she'd just earned,
A token from her spouse she said,
Her lover in a flash saw red.

ALR Loquitur

Pass me the mustard, Raymond;[1] I'm catching the train to
   Poole,
Where I'm due to present the prizes at the mental deficients'
   school.
Then I make a cross-country journey, via Crewe, to Bilston,
   Staffs,
Where I'm lecturing on my prose style and auctioning
   autographs.
Then I shall write an article to prove that *Horizon*'s absurd,
That Gibbon's[2] a second–rater and Stephen Spender's a
   turd.[3]
Then I shall do my broadcast on Martyn Skinner's[4] work,
And write to the papers explaining that Simmons[5] is greater
   than Burke.[6]

---

§ 'ALR speaks.' This evocation of A. L. Rowse (123/1) was found among
the papers of Isaiah Berlin, in an envelope postmarked 31 January 1947, which
may or may not be relevant to its date of composition. Rowse later referred to
Bowra's verses as 'brilliant and bawdy [. . .] an extraordinary production'
(journal entry for 8 June 1967, quoted by Richard Ollard in *A Man of
Contradictions*, 1999, 263), but perhaps that notoriously thin-skinned individual
had not seen this example. The poem has many similarities to John
Betjeman's 'How to Get on in Society', but it is not clear which was written
first. Betjeman's poem was first published in *Time and Tide* on 29 December
1951 as the subject of a competition, but was written no later than August
1949, when Randolph Churchill requested a copy.

   [1] Raymond Carr (b. 1919), Fellow of All Souls 1946–53; later Professor of
History of Latin America, Oxford, 1967–8 and Warden of St Antony's 1968–87.
   [2] Edward Gibbon (1737–94), historian, famous for his *The History of the
Decline and Fall of the Roman Empire* (1776–88).
   [3] Stephen Spender (33/2) founded and co-edited (with Cyril Connolly) the
literary magazine *Horizon* 1939–41.
   [4] Rowse, himself a poet, admired the craftsmanship displayed by the poet
Martyn Skinner (1906–93).
   [5] Rowse's friend Jack Simmons (1915–2000), Beit Lecturer in the History of
the British Empire, Oxford, 1943–47; Professor of History, Leicester, 1947–75.
   [6] Edmund Burke (1729–97), political thinker and statesman.

Do you think intellectuals in London can realise how sublime
Is the sparkling conversation at an All Souls breakfast-time?

I've tried to make them respect me; God only knows how I've
tried,
I've proved myself odder than Stoughton,[1] I've conquered
both time and tide,[2]
I'm poet, historian, critic – at politics I've done my bit.
I'm a genius, Raymond, a genius, but everyone says I'm a
shit.

---

[1] Perhaps a reference to Thomas Wilberforce Stoughton (1838–1911), co-founder of the publishing company Hodder and Stoughton, which had brought out Rowse's *The Use of History* in 1946.

[2] The political and literary magazine *Time and Tide* had been founded by Lady Rhondda in 1920. John Betjeman was its literary editor 1949–53, succeeding Rowse's friend Veronica Wedgwood; Rowse was a characteristically outspoken contributor.

'The wagtail waddles up the grass'

The wagtail waddles up the grass;
A planned regime has made him fat.
In the dishonest dusk he'd pass
For any self-made bureaucrat
Who's sat for years upon his arse.

The moon, who hikes across the sky,
Has lost her luggage on the way;
Green in the gills and none too spry,
She can't afford a holiday
With prices blowing up so high.

*Titanic*s vanish overnight
On icebergs planted like club bores;
Sharks blink in the electric light
And chew the carpets and the floors
To tickle up their appetite.

---

§ An undated typescript of this poem was found amongst Bowra's papers;
the physical format resembles those of poems known to have been his. Some
of the vocabulary suggests that Bowra composed at least a part of it. But if
the whole poem is by him, it is unlike anything else he is known to have
written. Apparently a love poem, in which descriptions of a disintegrating
world give way to a triumphant paean to the power of the narrator-lover and
the existence out of time of his love, it contains metaphysical conceits
reminiscent of John Donne and his contemporaries alongside passages with a
flavour of the 1930s. One possibility is that it is a joint composition: Bowra
belonged to an undergraduate circle of poets at New College (see p. xxiii
above) – although the poem's assurance and some of its internal references
suggest a later date than this – and continued playing poetry games with his
friends all his life. But if the author(s) and date of this poem remain (so far?)
mysterious, in literary quality the poem speaks for itself.

The blossoms on the Judas tree
Report a body black and burst;
From writhing boughs the blood flows free
To prove that guilt is not the worst
Thing that can trouble you and me.

As balanced as a billiard-cue,
Unpunctual as April rain,
My appetite comes back to you.
And though it may not come again,
It knows the job it has to do.

The bodies of the bygone years,
Sunk in their secret Passchendaeles,[1]
Swing to the surface, their dead ears
Deaf to the thousand nightingales
Who mock the irony of tears.

The Obi and the Yenisei[2]
Roll down their corpse-encumbered streams
To tundras by the polar sea,
But my disaster-clotted dreams
Spout skyward like a ginkgo tree.[3]

No daddy-long-legs skips about
With so insensate a delight;
No pike plots ambush for a trout
With so delirious a spite
As I do with my hackles out.

---

[1] The Third Battle of Ypres (31 July to 6 November 1917), called
Passchendaele after the village whose capture brought to an end one of the
bloodiest and muddiest battles of the First World War; Bowra took part in the
later stages, and his experiences there, recounted in his *Memories*, marked him
for life.

[2] Rivers in Siberia, convenient places to dispose of the victims of the
Russian Civil War (1918–20) and of Stalin's Gulag.

[3] There were ginkgos in Wadham gardens, of which Bowra always spoke
with affection, partly because the ginkgo was so ancient a variety of tree,
partly (perhaps) because of its Chinese connections with his youth.

No anaconda stuffed with goat
And gurgling round and round a tree
Has such a warble in his throat
As I, when gaily on the sea,
Like halcyons my fancies float.

I'm Halley's Comet come again
Through the ineptitudes of space,
And flap my incandescent train
Into the sun's flat Sunday face
And shut him up if he complain.

Aurora Borealis lights
Her feeble gas-jets in the sky;
I break the Seven Sleepers'[1] nights
With huge atomic arcs as I
Shoot salvoed moons in rainbow flights.

My shameless appetite will beat
The termite gnawing in the door
To satisfy his taste for sweat;
Or cockroach scrabbling on the floor
For scabs of snot and spunk to eat.

The scrotum-bellied octopus
May spew his filthy ink around;
Appalled by his malignant fuss,
The lesser fry are stunned and drowned,
But he'll not dare to trouble us.

---

[1] According to legend, seven Christian youths from Ephesus fled to a cave
to escape persecution, and slept there for hundreds of years.

I am a Pope who tells no lies,
A Dalai Lama on his throne,
Incarnate wisdom of the wise,
Who, stiff, unprompted and alone,
Lay down the dogma of the skies.

I am a greasy Aztec god,
A grin upon a totem-pole,
And where the earthbound footsteps plod,
I rip the body from the soul
And make it dance upon the sod.

From the skyscraper of my bones
Look out a thousand thousand eyes,
And in my nerves the telephones
Buzz with rude questions and replies
Instead of pompous semitones.

Go-getting goblins and grim ghouls,
Who used to block the corridors,
Have left their files and piles and stools
To spend their Whitsun out of doors
Next to the Paradise of Fools.

On top beside the wireless mast
My expectation looks to sea;
It sees the steamers dawdling past,
With cargoes packed for you and me;
My hawsers swoop and make them fast.

It hears the snorting Underground
Rumble its bellyful and hears
Electric circles waltzing round
The civic bandstand of the spheres,
Respectful of the rate-paid sound.

Through every pore, through every vein,
Through every artery the crowd
Of tourists in my body strain
Myopic eyes towards the loud
Lights in the nightclub of my brain.

The sky is poured down from above
Like water from a dark-blue stream;
It turns the town to treasure-trove
And makes its dusty gewgaws gleam
Like jewels from the vaults of love.

White bodies bathing in a lake
Are lit with phosphorescent stars
And flushed with lightnings where the break
Of currents sweeps across the bars
In waterflaps and waterflake.

Stars, bathing in the Milky Way,
Turn somersaults in creamy foam,
Or ride the surf of dawning day;
Meteors indolently roam
In skiffs of dusk across the bay.

Before a million years went by,
In the coal-forest's redwood trees
A dragonfly and dragonfly
Floated in unreflective ease,
And one was you, and one was I.

Index of names

COMPILED BY DOUGLAS MATTHEWS